Please return to!

Wally Shsatta

707-584-8310

Hymns II

*edited by Paul Beckwith,
Hughes Huffman & Mark Hunt*

*InterVarsity Press
Downers Grove
Illinois 60515*

InterVarsity Press is the book-publishing division of Inter-Varsity Christian Fellowship, a student movement active on campus at hundreds of universities, colleges and schools of nursing. For information about local and regional activities, write IVCF, 233 Langdon St., Madison, WI 53703.

All Scripture quotations, unless otherwise indicated, are from the Revised Standard Version of the Bible, copyrighted 1946, 1952, © 1971 and 1973 by the Division of Christian Education of the National Council of the Churches of Christ, and are used by permission.

Paper ISBN 0-87784-783-5
Cloth ISBN 0-87784-898-X
Spiral ISBN 0-87784-750-9

Library of Congress Catalog Card Number: 76-47503

Printed in the United States of America

Hymns II is published in paper, cloth and spiral editions. Please specify when ordering.

22   21   20   19   18   17   16   15   14   13   12
96   95   94   93   92

Contents

Martin Bucer, an early German reformer, once stated that the Church is built around the hymn. It is with great consciousness of this historic role of hymns within the Church that we have produced this hymnal.

Recent events have also played a part in molding this collection, for this is the first hymnal or songbook published by InterVarsity Press not primarily under the editorship of Paul Beckwith. Paul assisted us in the early stages of this project, but the Lord called him into his presence shortly after the initial groundwork for this book was laid. Although his absence has been keenly felt, we trust that this hymnal will follow in the Beckwith tradition of strong music coupled with theologically sound texts.

Unlike its predecessor, *Hymns II* is structured by subject. This has enabled us to strengthen traditionally weak hymn topics such as the Holy Spirit, the Church, and Scripture. Deciding upon a single subject for many hymns is nearly impossible, and so we encourage users to go beyond the sections we have provided when selecting hymns on a particular theme.

Other indexes have been added to make the hymnal more useable. The *scripture index* attempts to tie the hymns to biblical passages from which the idea of the hymn was taken. This is often not clearly indicated by the author, and thus our references should not be considered complete or final. Hymns known to be based upon a particular passage are noted with an asterisk (*) in the index. Scriptural quotations appearing with the hymns have been taken from the Revised Standard Version. The *metrical index* groups tunes by meters, allowing music to be interchanged with any texts of the same meter. For example, "For Your Gift of God the Spirit" (No. 76) can also be sung to the tune of "What a Friend We Have in Jesus" (No. 139). Not all tunes of the same meter will match the feeling of the texts, but often a well known text can be brought to life with a new tune. Tune names are helpful when mixing tunes and words, so we have included an index of *tune names.* Finally, from time to time you will find the *author/composer* indexes helpful in tracing down a particular hymn.

Guitar chords have been included with most of the music. We have endeavored to keep the chords as simple as possible. In order to accomplish this it has been necessary, at times, to put the chords in a different key from the music. There is *no* notation of this in the music, but this should cause no difficulties unless other instruments are used. Parenthetical chords should be considered optional. A close examination of the texts will reveal unusual hyphenations. We have attempted to divide words in a way which provides proper pronunciation for singing and yet renders words easily recognizable. This middle road is hard to follow, but, we trust, appealing to user, poet and musician alike. Every effort has been made to obtain proper copyrights. Any errors or omissions are unintentional and will be corrected in subsequent editions.

We wish to thank the many people who have assisted us in this project, especially Michael Baughen and Timothy Dudley-Smith for their help with the *Psalm Praise* material. May this book be used to the glory of God!

"O sing to the LORD a new song; sing to the LORD, all the earth!" (Ps. 96:1)

Mark Hunt/Hughes Huffman

God the Father

Immortal, invisible, God only wise,
In light inaccessible hid from our eyes,
Most blessed, most glorious, the Ancient of Days,
Almighty, victorious, Thy great name we praise.
Walter C Smith

1   Praise to the Lord, the Almighty

God the Father

... you will delight yourself in the Almighty/Job 22:26

Joachim Neander (1650-1680)
tr Catherine Winkworth (1827-1878)

"Stralsund Gesangbuch" (1665)
Lobe Den Herren   14 14 4 7 8

1. Praise to the Lord, the Al-might-y, the King of cre-a-tion!
2. Praise to the Lord! who o'er all things so won-drous-ly reign-eth,
3. Praise to the Lord! who doth pros-per thy work and de-fend thee;
4. Praise to the Lord! O let all that is in me a-dore Him!

O my soul, praise Him, for He is thy health and sal-va-tion!
Shel-ters thee un-der His wings, yea, so gent-ly su-stain-eth;
Sure-ly His good-ness and mer-cy here dai-ly at-tend thee.
All that hath life and breath, come now with prais-es be-fore Him!

All ye who hear, Now to His tem-ple draw near;
Hast thou not seen How thy en-treat-ies have been
Pon-der a-new What the Al-might-y can do,
Let the A-men Sound from His peo-ple a-gain;

Praise Him in glad a-do-ra-tion!
Grant-ed in what He or-dain-eth?
If with His love He be-friend thee.
Glad-ly for aye we a-dore Him. A-men.

2   O Worship the King   God the Father

O LORD my God, thou art very great/Ps 104:1

Robert Grant (1779-1838)

William Croft (1678-1727)
Hanover   5 5 5 5 6 5 6 5

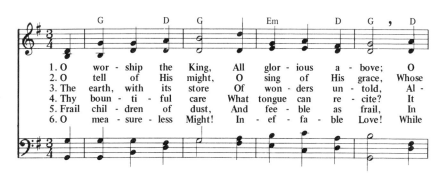

1. O   wor - ship   the   King,   All   glor - ious   a - bove;   O
2. O   tell   of   His   might,   O   sing   of   His   grace,   Whose
3. The   earth,   with   its   store   Of   won - ders   un - told,   Al -
4. Thy   boun - ti - ful   care   What   tongue   can   re - cite?   It
5. Frail   chil - dren   of   dust,   And   fee - ble   as   frail,   In
6. O   mea - sure - less   Might!   In - ef - fa - ble   Love!   While

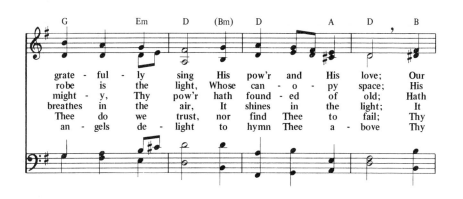

grate - ful - ly   sing   His   pow'r   and   His   love;   Our
robe   is   the   light,   Whose   can - o - py   space;   His
might - y,   Thy   pow'r   hath   found - ed   of   old;   Hath
breathes   in   the   air,   It   shines   in   the   light;   It
Thee   do   we   trust,   nor   find   Thee   to   fail;   Thy
an - gels   de - light   to   hymn   Thee   a - bove,   Thy

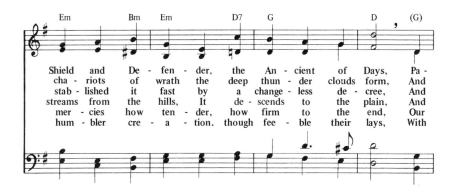

Shield   and   De - fen - der,   the   An - cient   of   Days,   Pa -
cha - riots   of   wrath   the   deep   thun - der   clouds   form,   And
stab - lished   it   fast   by   a   change - less   de - cree,   And
streams   from   the   hills,   It   de - scends   to   the   plain,   And
mer - cies   how   ten - der,   how   firm   to   the   end,   Our
hum - bler   cre - a - tion,   though   fee - ble   their   lays,   With

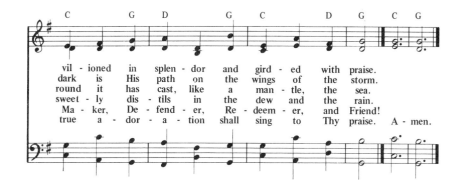

C	G	D	G	C	D	G	C	G

vil - ioned in splen - dor and gird - ed with praise.
dark is His path on the wings of the storm.
round it has cast, like a man - tle, the sea.
sweet - ly dis - tils in the dew and the rain.
Ma - ker, De - fend - er, Re - deem - er, and Friend!
true a - dor - a - tion shall sing to Thy praise. A - men.

3 **Stand Up, and Bless the Lord**   God the Father
Stand up and bless the LORD your God/Neh 9:5

James Montgomery (1771-1854)   *Charles Lockhart (1745-1815)*
descant by Sydney Hugo Nicholson (1875-1947)
Carlisle   6 6 8 6

Descant

E   A   B   E   A   E   E/B   B

1. Stand up, and bless the Lord, Ye peo - ple of His choice;
2. Though high a - bove all praise, A - bove all bles - sing high,
3. O for the liv - ing flame From His own al - tar brought,
4. God is our strength and song, And His sal - va - tion ours;
5. Stand up, and bless the Lord, The Lord your God a - dore;

E   F#m   E/G#   A   (B7)   E   A   E/B   B7   E   A   D

Stand up, and bless the Lord, your God With heart and soul and voice.
Who would not fear His ho - ly name, And praise and mag - ni - fy?
To touch our lips, our minds in - spire, And wing to heav'n our thought!
Then be His love in Christ pro-claimed With all our ran-somed pow'rs.
Stand up, and bless His glo - rious name Hence-forth for - e - ver-more. A-men.

4 **Praise Him, Praise Him**

God the Father

Praise the LORD from the heavens/Ps 148:1

Michael Perry

Kenneth Coates
12 13 12 10

1. Praise Him, praise Him, praise Him! pow'rs and do-mi-na-tions,
2. Praise Him, praise Him, praise Him! o-cean depths and wa-ters,
3. Praise Him, praise Him, praise Him! men of God who fear Him:

Praise His Name in glo-rious light, you crea-tures of the day!
E-le-ments of earth and heav'n, your sev-'ral prais-es blend.
To the high-est Name of all, con-cert-ed an-thems raise —

Moon and stars ring prais-es through the con-stel-la-tions:
Birds and beasts and cat-tle, Ad-am's sons and daugh-ters,
All you sons of Is-rael, ho-ly peo-ple near Him

Lord God, whose word shall ne-ver pass a-way.
Wor-ship the King whose reign shall ne-ver end!
Whom He ex-alts to pow'r and crowns with praise. A-men.

5   Immortal, Invisible, God Only Wise   God the Father

To the . . . immortal, invisible, the only God, be honor and glory/1 Tim 1:17

Walter C Smith (1824-1908)

Welsh Melody
Roberts' "Caniadau y Cyssegr" (1839)
St Denio   11   11   11   11

1. Im - mor - tal, in - vi - si - ble, God on - ly wise,
2. Un - rest - ing, un - hast - ing, and si - lent as light,
3. To all, life thou giv - est, to both great and small;
4. Great Fa - ther of glo - ry, pure Fa - ther of light,

In light in - ac - ces - si - ble hid from our eyes,
Nor want - ing, nor wast - ing, thou rul - est in might;
In all life thou liv - est, the true life of all;
Thine an - gels a - dore thee, all veil - ing their sight;

Most bles - sed, most glo - rious, the An - cient of Days,
Thy jus - tice like moun - tains high soar - ing a - bove
We blos - som and flou - rish as leaves on the tree,
All praise we would ren - der: O help us to see

Al - might - y, vic - to - rious, thy great name we praise.
Thy clouds, which are foun - tains of good - ness and love.
And wi - ther and per - ish but naught chang - eth thee.
'Tis on - ly the splen - dor of light hid - eth thee. A - men.

6   **Give to Our God Immortal Praise**   God the Father

...for his steadfast love endures for ever/Ps 136:1

Isaac Watts (1674-1748)

"Geistliche Kirchengesang" Cologne (1623)
arr and harm by Ralph Vaughan Williams (1872-1958)
Lasst Uns Erfreuen 8 8 8 8 w/Hallelujahs

1. Give to our God im - mor - tal praise!   Mer - cy and truth are all His
2. Give to the Lord of lords re - nown,   The   King of kings with glo - ry
3. He   saw the Gen-tiles dead in sin,   And   felt his pi - ty work with-
4. He   sent His Son with pow'r to save,   From   guilt, and dark-ness, and the

ways;   Al - le - lu - ia! Al - le - lu - ia! Won - ders of grace to God be-
crown;   Al - le - lu - ia! Al - le - lu - ia! His   mer - cies e - ver shall en-
in;   Al - le - lu - ia! Al - le - lu - ia! His   mer - cies e - ver shall en-
grave;   Al - le - lu - ia! Al - le - lu - ia! Won - ders of grace to God be-

long,   Re - peat His mer - cies in your song.   Al - le - lu - ia! Al - le -
dure,   When lords and kings are known no more.   Al - le - lu - ia! Al - le -
dure,   When death and sin shall reign no more.   Al - le - lu - ia! Al - le -
long,   Re - peat His mer - cies in your song.   Al - le - lu - ia! Al - le -

lu - ia! Al - le - lu - ia! Al - le - lu - ia! Al - le - lu - ia!   A - men.

I Sing the Mighty Power of God

God the Father

O come, let us worship . . . let us kneel before the LORD, our Maker!/Ps 95:6

Isaac Watts (1674-1748)

"*Gesangbuch der Herzogl*" *Wirtemberg (1784)*
Ellacombe   8 6 8 6 D

1. I sing the might-y pow'r of God, That made the moun-tains rise;
2. I sing the good-ness of the Lord, That filled the earth with food;
3. There's not a plant or flow'r be-low, But makes Thy glo-ries known:

That spread the flow-ing seas a-broad, And built the loft-y skies.
He formed the crea-tures with His word, And then pro-nounced them good.
And clouds a-rise, and tem-pests blow, By or-der from Thy throne;

I sing the wis-dom that or-dained The sun to rule the day;
Lord, how Thy won-ders are dis-played, Wher-e'er I turn my eye:
While all that bor-rows life from Thee Is e-ver in Thy care.

The moon shines full at His com-mand, And all the stars o-bey.
If I sur-vey the ground I tread, Or gaze up-on the sky!
And e-v'ry-where that man can be, Thou, God, art pres-ent there. A-men.

8   The God of Abraham Praise

God the Father

My praise is continually of thee/Ps 71:6

Yigdal of Daniel ben Judah (c1400)
Thomas Olivers (1725-1799)

Hebrew Melody
arr Meyer Lyon (1751-1799)
Leoni   6 6 8 4 D

1. The God of A-br'ham praise, Who reigns en-throned a-bove;
2. The God of A-br'ham praise, At whose su-preme com-mand
3. He by Him-self hath sworn, I on His oath de-pend,
4. The whole tri-um-phant host Give thanks to God on high;

An-cient of e-ver-last-ing days, And God of love.
From earth I rise, and seek the joys At His right hand.
I shall, on ea-gles' wings up-borne, To heav'n a-scend;
"Hail, Fa-ther, Son and Ho-ly Ghost!" They e-ver cry.

Je-ho-vah, great I AM, By earth and heav'n con-fessed;
I all on earth for-sake, Its wis-dom, fame, and pow'r;
I shall be-hold His face, I shall His pow'r a-dore,
Hail, A-br'ham's God and mine! I join the heav'n-ly lays;

I bow and bless the sa-cred name, For-e-ver blest.
And Him my on-ly por-tion make, My shield and tow'r.
And sing the won-ders of His grace For-e-ver-more.
All might and ma-jes-ty are Thine, And end-less praise. A-men.

Praise, My Soul

God the Father

Bless the LORD, O my soul, and forget not all his benefits/Ps 103:2

Henry F Lyte (1793-1847)

John Goss (1800-1880)
Lauda Anima 8 7 8 7 8 7

1. Praise, my soul, the King of hea - ven, To His feet your
2. Praise Him for His grace and fa - vor To our fa - thers
3. Fa - ther - like, He tends and spares us, Well our fee - ble
4. An - gels help us to a - dore Him, You be - hold Him

tri - bute bring; Ran - somed, healed, re - stored, for - gi - ven,
in dis - tress; Praise Him, still the same for e - ver,
frame He knows; In His hands He gen - tly bears us,
face to face; Sun and moon, bow down be - fore Him;

Who, like me, His praise should sing? Al - le - lu - ia!
Slow to chide, and swift to bless; Al - le - lu - ia!
Res - cues us from all our foes; Al - le - lu - ia!
Dwel - lers all in time and space, Al - le - lu - ia!

Al - le - lu - ia! Praise the e - ver - last - ing King!
Al - le - lu - ia! Glo - rious in His faith - ful - ness!
Al - le - lu - ia! Wide - ly as His mer - cy flows!
Al - le - lu - ia! Praise with us the God of grace! A - men

Holy, holy, holy, is the Lord God Almighty/Rev 4:8

Reginald Heber (1783-1826)

John B Dykes (1823-1876)
Nicaea 11 12 12 10

1. Ho-ly, ho-ly, ho-ly! Lord God Al-might-y!
Ear-ly in the morn-ing our song shall rise to Thee;
Ho-ly, ho-ly, ho-ly! mer-ci-ful and might-y!
God in three per-sons, bles-sed Tri-ni-ty!

2. Ho-ly, ho-ly, ho-ly! all the saints a-dore Thee,
Cast-ing down their gold-en crowns a-round the glas-sy sea;
Cher-u-bim and ser-a-phim fal-ling down be-fore Thee,
Who wert and art and e-ver more shalt be.

3. Ho-ly, ho-ly, ho-ly! though the dark-ness hide Thee,
Though the eye of sin-ful man Thy glo-ry may not see,
On-ly Thou art ho-ly; there is none be-side Thee,
Per-fect in pow'r, in love, and pu-ri-ty.

4. Ho-ly, ho-ly, ho-ly! Lord God Al-might-y!
All Thy works shall praise Thy name, in earth, and sky, and sea;
Ho-ly, ho-ly, ho-ly! mer-ci-ful and might-y!
God in three per-sons, bles-sed Tri-ni-ty! A-men.

11   A Mighty Fortress Is Our God

God the Father

God is our refuge and strength/Ps 46:1

Martin Luther (1483-1546)
tr Frederick H Hedge (1805-1890)

Martin Luther (1483-1546)
Ein' Feste Burg   8 7 8 7 6 6 6 6 7

1. A might-y For-tress is our God, A Bul-wark ne-ver fail - ing;
2. Did we in our own strength con-fide, Our striv-ing would be los - ing;
3. And though this world, with de-vils filled, Should threat-en to un-do us;
4. That word a-bove all earth-ly pow'rs, No thanks to them a-bi - deth;

Our Help-er He a-mid the flood Of mor-tal ills pre-vail - ing:
Were not the right Man on our side, The Man of God's own choos - ing:
We will not fear, for God hath willed His truth to tri-umph through us:
The Spi-rit and the gifts are ours Through Him who with us sid - eth:

For still our an-cient Foe Doth seek to work us woe; His craft and pow'r are great,
Dost ask who that may be? Christ Je-sus, it is He; Lord Sab-a-oth His Name,
The Prince of Dark-ness grim, We trem-ble not for him; His rage we can en-dure,
Let goods and kin-dred go, This mor-tal life al-so; The bo-dy they may kill;

And, armed with cru-el hate, On earth is not his e-qual.
From age to age the same, And He must win the bat-tle.
For lo! his doom is sure, One lit-tle word shall fell him.
God's truth a-bi-deth still, His King-dom is for-e-ver. A-men.

12 Great Is Thy Faithfulness

God the Father

... his mercies never come to an end; they are new every morning/Lam 3:22, 23

Thomas O Chisholm (1866-1960)

William M Runyan (1870-1957)
Faithfulness 11 10 11 10 w/refrain

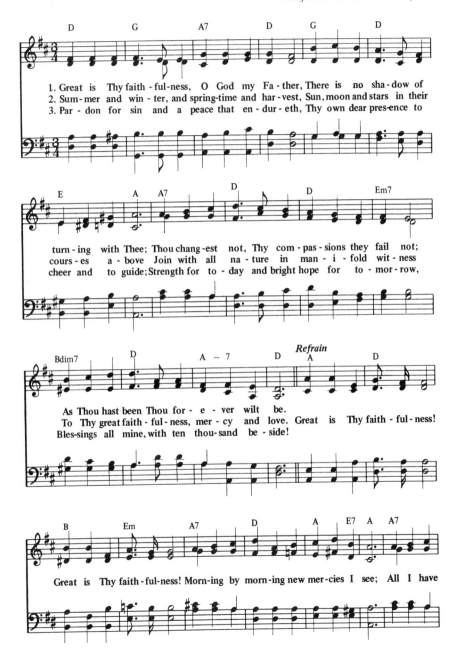

1. Great is Thy faith-ful-ness, O God my Fa-ther, There is no sha-dow of
2. Sum-mer and win-ter, and spring-time and har-vest, Sun, moon and stars in their
3. Par-don for sin and a peace that en-dur-eth, Thy own dear pres-ence to

turn-ing with Thee; Thou chang-est not, Thy com-pas-sions they fail not;
cours-es a-bove Join with all na-ture in man-i-fold wit-ness
cheer and to guide; Strength for to-day and bright hope for to-mor-row,

Refrain

As Thou hast been Thou for-e-ver wilt be.
To Thy great faith-ful-ness, mer-cy and love. Great is Thy faith-ful-ness!
Bles-sings all mine, with ten thou-sand be-side!

Great is Thy faith-ful-ness! Morn-ing by morn-ing new mer-cies I see; All I have

needed Thy hand hath pro-vid-ed—Great is Thy faith-ful-ness,Lord,un-to me! A-men.

13 God the Omnipotent

God the Father

For the LORD, the Most High, is terrible, a great king/Ps 47:2

Henry Charley (1808-1872) sts 1, 2
John Ellerton (1826-1893) sts 3, 4

Alexis F Lvov (1799-1870)
Russian Hymn 11 10 11 9

1. God the Om-ni-po-tent, King, who or-dain-est Thun-der thy
2. God the All mer-ci-ful, earth hath for-sak-en Thy ways all
3. God the All right-eous One, man hath de-fied thee, Yet to e-
4. God the All prov-i-dent, earth by thy chas-t'ning Yet shall to

cla-rion, the light-ning thy sword, Show forth thy pi-ty on high where thou
ho-ly, and slight-ed thy word; Bid not thy wrath in its ter-rors a-
ter-ni-ty stand-eth thy word; False-hood and wrong shall not tar-ry be-
free-dom and truth be re-stored; Thru the thick dark-ness thy king-dom is

reign-est: Give to us peace in our time, O Lord.
wak-en: Give to us peace in our time, O Lord.
side thee: Give to us peace in our time, O Lord.
has-t'ning: Thou wilt give peace in thy time, O Lord. A-men.

14 God, All Nature Sings Thy Glory

God the Father

O LORD, how manifold are thy works!/Ps 104:24

David Clowney

Ludwig van Beethoven (1770-1827)
Ode to Joy 8 7 8 7 D

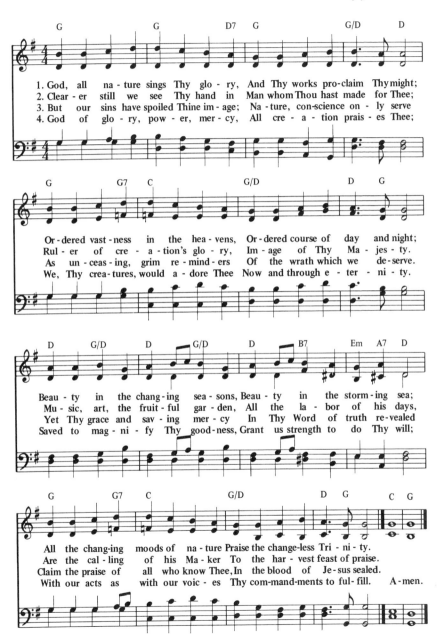

1. God, all na-ture sings Thy glo-ry, And Thy works pro-claim Thy might;
2. Clear-er still we see Thy hand in Man whom Thou hast made for Thee;
3. But our sins have spoiled Thine im-age; Na-ture, con-science on-ly serve
4. God of glo-ry, pow-er, mer-cy, All cre-a-tion prais-es Thee;

Or-dered vast-ness in the hea-vens, Or-dered course of day and night;
Rul-er of cre-a-tion's glo-ry, Im-age of Thy Ma-jes-ty.
As un-ceas-ing, grim re-mind-ers Of the wrath which we de-serve.
We, Thy crea-tures, would a-dore Thee Now and through e-ter-ni-ty.

Beau-ty in the chang-ing sea-sons, Beau-ty in the storm-ing sea;
Mu-sic, art, the fruit-ful gar-den, All the la-bor of his days,
Yet Thy grace and sav-ing mer-cy In Thy Word of truth re-vealed
Saved to mag-ni-fy Thy good-ness, Grant us strength to do Thy will;

All the chang-ing moods of na-ture Praise the change-less Tri-ni-ty.
Are the cal-ling of his Ma-ker To the har-vest feast of praise.
Claim the praise of all who know Thee, In the blood of Je-sus sealed.
With our acts as with our voic-es Thy com-mand-ments to ful-fill. A-men.

15   O God of Every Nation

God the Father

. . . for thou dost judge the peoples with equity and guide the nations/Ps 67:4

William W Reid Jr (1923-   )

Hughes M Huffman (1942-   )
Creation Prayer   7 6 7 6 D

1. O God of ev'ry nation, Of ev'ry race and land,
Redeem thy whole creation With thine almighty hand:
Where hate and fear divide us And bitter threats are hurled,
In love and mercy guide us, And heal our strife-torn world.

2. From search for wealth and power And scorn of truth and right,
From trust in bombs that shower Destruction thru the night,
From pride of race and station And blindness to thy way,
Deliver ev'ry nation, Eternal God, we pray.

3. Lord, strengthen all who labor That men may find release
From fear of rattling saber, From dread of war's increase:
When hope and courage falter, Thy still, small voice be heard;
With faith that none can alter, Thy servants undergird.

4. Keep bright in us the vision Of days when war shall cease,
When hatred and division Give way to love and peace,
Till dawns the morning glorious When brotherhood shall reign,
And Christ shall rule victorious O'er all the world's domain.

A-men.

To God Be the Glory

Ascribe to the LORD the glory of his name/Ps 29:2

Fanny J Crosby (1820-1915)

William H Doane (1832-1915)
To God Be The Glory 11 11 11 11 w/refrain

1. To God be the glo - ry, great things He hath done, So lov'd He the
2. Oh, per - fect re - demp - tion, the pur-chase of blood, To e - v'ry be -
3. Great things He hath taught us, great things He hath done, And great our re -

world that He gave us His Son, Who yield - ed His life an a -
liev - er the pro - mise of God; The vil - est of - fend - er who
joic - ing thro' Je - sus the Son; But pur - er, and high - er, and

tone-ment for sin, And o - pened the Life Gate that all may go in.
tru - ly be - lieves, That mo - ment from Je - sus a par - don re - ceives.
great - er will be Our won - der, our trans - port when Je - sus we see.

Refrain

Praise the Lord, praise the Lord, let the earth hear His voice; Praise the

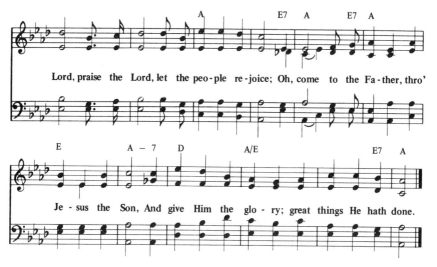

Lord, praise the Lord, let the peo-ple re-joice; Oh, come to the Fa-ther, thro'

Je-sus the Son, And give Him the glo-ry; great things He hath done.

17   My God, How Wonderful Thou Art   God the Father

... the high and lofty One who inhabits eternity, whose name is Holy/Is 57:15

Frederick W Faber (1814-1863)

James Turle (1802-1882)
Westminster 8 6 8 6

1. My God, how won-der-ful Thou art, Thy ma-jes-ty how bright,
2. How dread are Thine e-ter-nal years, O e-ver-last-ing Lord,
3. O, how I fear Thee, liv-ing God, With deep-est, ten-d'rest fears,
4. Yet I may love Thee too, O Lord, Al-might-y as Thou art,
5. No earth-ly fa-ther loves like Thee; No mo-ther e'er so mild,
6. How won-der-ful, how beau-ti-ful, The sight of Thee must be,

How beau-ti-ful Thy mer-cy seat, In depths of burn-ing light!
By pros-trate spi-rits day and night In-ces-sant-ly a-dored!
And wor-ship Thee with trem-bling hope And pen-i-ten-tial tears!
For Thou hast stooped to ask of me The love of my poor heart!
Bears and for-bears as Thou hast done with me, Thy sin-ful child.
Thine end-less wis-dom, bound-less pow'r, And awe-ful pur-i-ty! A-men.

18 Be Thou My Vision

God the Father

But whatever gain I had, I counted as loss for the sake of Christ/Phil 3:7

Ancient Irish
tr Eleanor H Hull (1860-1935)
versified by Mary E Byrne (1880-1931)

Irish Melody
Harmonized by Hughes M Huffman (1942-   )
Slane   10 10 10 10 Irreg Dactylic

1. Be Thou my Vi - sion, O Lord of my heart;
2. Be Thou my Wis - dom, and Thou my true Word;
3. Be Thou my bat - tle shield, sword for my fight;
4. Rich - es I heed not, nor man's emp - ty praise,
5. High King of hea - ven, my vic - to - ry won,

Naught be all else to me, save that Thou art —
I e - ver with Thee and Thou with me, Lord;
Be Thou my dig - ni - ty, Thou my de - light,
Thou mine in - her - i - tance, now and al - ways:
May I reach hea - ven's joys, O bright heav'n's Son!

Thou my best thought by day or by night,
Thou my great Fa - ther, I Thy true son;
Thou my soul's shel - ter, Thou my high tow'r:
Thou and Thou on - ly, first in my heart,
Heart of my own heart, What - e - ver be - fall,

Wak - ing or sleep - ing, Thy pres - ence my light.
Thou in me dwel - ling, and I with Thee one.
Raise Thou me heav'n - ward, O Pow'r of my pow'r.
High King of hea - ven, my Trea - sure Thou art.
Still be my Vi - sion, O Rul - er of all.

19 I'll Praise My Maker

God the Father

I will praise the LORD as long as I live/Ps 146:2

Isaac Watts (1674-1748)

Gabriel Davis (c1768-1824)
Monmouth 8 8 8 8 8 8

1. I'll praise my Ma-ker while I've breath; And when my voice is lost in death, Praise shall em-ploy my no-bler pow'rs; My days of praise shall ne'er be past, While life, and thought, and be-ing last, Or im-mor-ta-li-ty en-dures.

2. Hap-py the man whose hopes re-ly On Is-rael's God! He made the sky, And earth, and sea, with all their train: His truth for e-ver stands se-cure; He saves the op-pressed, He feeds the poor, And none shall find His pro-mise vain.

3. The Lord gives eye-sight to the blind; The Lord sup-ports the faint-ing mind; He sends the la-b'ring con-science peace; He helps the stran-ger in dis-tress, The wid-ow and the fa-ther-less And grants the pri-s'ner sweet re-lease.

4. I'll praise Him while He lends me breath; And when my voice is lost in death, Praise shall em-ploy my no-bler pow'rs; My days of praise shall ne'er be past, While life, and thought, and be-ing last, Or im-mor-ta-li-ty en-dures. A-men.

20   Great God of Wonders

Who is a God like thee, pardoning iniquity . . . ?/Mic 7:18

Samuel Davies (1723-1761)

John Newton
Sovereignty 8 8 8 8 w/refrain

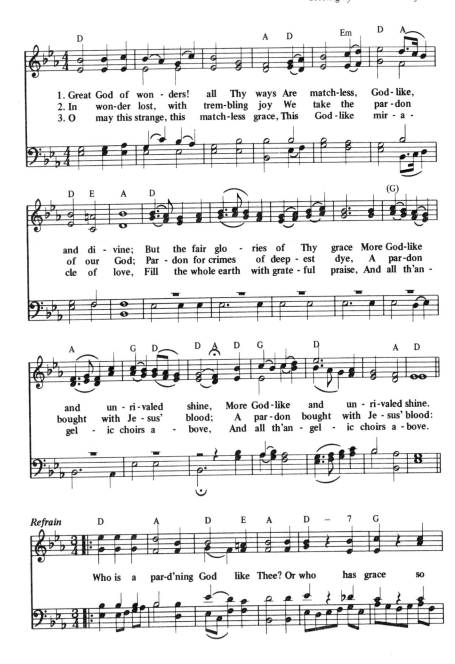

1. Great God of won - ders! all Thy ways Are match-less, God - like, and di - vine; But the fair glo - ries of Thy grace More God-like and un - ri - valed shine, More God-like and un - ri - valed shine.

2. In won-der lost, with trem-bling joy We take the par - don of our God; Par - don for crimes of deep - est dye, A par - don bought with Je - sus' blood; A par - don bought with Je - sus' blood:

3. O may this strange, this match-less grace, This God - like mir - a - cle of love, Fill the whole earth with grate - ful praise, And all th'an - gel - ic choirs a - bove, And all th'an - gel - ic choirs a - bove.

Refrain

Who is a par-d'ning God like Thee? Or who has grace so

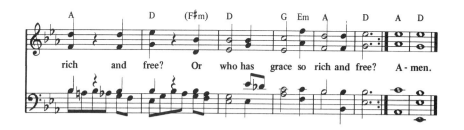

rich and free? Or who has grace so rich and free? A - men.

21 **Eternal Light! Eternal Light!**

God the Father

His brightness was like the light/Hab 3:4

Thomas Binney (1798-1874)

Frederick C Maker (1844-1927)
Rest 8 6 8 8 6

1. E - ter - nal Light! E - ter - nal Light! How pure the soul must
2. The spi - rits that sur - round Thy throne May bear the burn - ing
3. Oh, how shall I, whose na - tive sphere Is dark, whose mind is
4. There is a way for man to rise To that sub - lime a -
5. These, these pre - pare us for the sight Of ho - li - ness a -

be When, placed with - in Thy search - ing sight, It shrinks not, but with
bliss; But that is sure - ly theirs a - lone, Since they have ne - ver,
dim, Be - fore th' In - ef - fa - ble ap - pear, And on my na - ked
bode; An Of - f'ring and a Sac - ri - fice, A Ho - ly Spi - rit's
bove; The sons of ig - no - rance and night May dwell in the E -

calm de - light Can live, and look on Thee!
ne - ver known A fal - len world like this.
spi - rit bear The un - cre - at - ed beam?
en - er - gies, An Ad - vo - cate with God:
ter - nal Light, Thro' the E - ter - nal Love. A - men.

God the Son: *His glory, name, and praise*

O Jesus, King most wonderful, Thou Conqueror renowned;
Thou Sweetness most ineffable, In whom all joys are found;
Thee may our tongues forever bless; Thee may we love alone;
And ever in our lives express the image of Thine own.

Bernard of Clairvaux

22 We Come, O Christ to Thee   His Glory, Name, & Praise

I am the way, and the truth, and the life/Jn 14:6

E Margaret Clarkson (1915-   )

John Darwall (1731-1789)
Darwall 6 6 6 6 8 8

1. We come, O Christ, to Thee, True Son of God and man, By Whom all things con - sist, In Whom all life be - gan: In Thee a - lone we live and move, And have our be - ing in Thy love.
2. Thou art the Way to God, Thy blood our ran - som paid; In Thee we face our Judge And Mak - er un - a - fraid. Be - fore the throne ab - solved we stand, Thy love has met Thy law's de - mand.
3. Thou art the liv - ing Truth! All wis - dom dwells in Thee, Thou Source of e - v'ry skill, E - ter - nal Ver - i - ty! Thou great I Am! In Thee we rest, True an - swer to our e - v'ry quest.
4. Thou on - ly art true Life, To know Thee is to live The more a - bun - dant life That earth can ne - ver give: O ris - en Lord! We live in Thee, And Thou in us e - ter - nal - ly.
5. We wor - ship Thee, Lord Christ, Our Sa - vior and our King, To Thee our youth and strength A - dor - ing - ly we bring: So fill our hearts, that men may see Thy life in us, and turn to Thee. A - men.

23 Jesus, Priceless Treasure

His Glory, Name, & Praise

Peace I leave with you; my peace I give to you/Jn 14:27

Johann Franck (1618-1677)
tr Catherine Winkworth (1827-1878)

German melody
arr J S Bach (1685-1750)
Jesu, Meine Freude 6 6 5 6 6 5 7 8 6

1. Je - sus, price-less trea - sure; Source of pur-est plea - sure,
2. In thine arm I rest me; Foes who would mo - lest me
3. Hence, all thoughts of sad - ness! For the Lord of glad - ness,

Tru - est friend to me: Long my heart hath pant - ed, Till it well-nigh
Can - not reach me here. Though the earth be shak - ing, E - v'ry heart be
Je - sus, en - ters in. Those who love the Fa - ther, Though the storm may

faint - ed, Thirst-ing af - ter thee. Thine I am, O spot-less Lamb,
quak - ing, God dis-pels our fear. Sin and hell in con-flict fell
ga - ther, Still have peace with - in. Yea, what-e'er we must here bear,

I will suf-fer nought to hide thee, Ask for nought be-side thee.
With their heav-iest storm as - sail us; Je-sus will not fail us;
Still in thee lies pur-est plea - sure, Je-sus price-less trea - sure.

24 None Other Lamb

His Glory, Name, & Praise

Whom have I in heaven but thee?/Ps 73:25

Christina G Rossetti (1830-1894)

Peggy S Palmer (1900-   )
Ellasgarth   8 10 10 4

Descant   3. Lord, Thou art life, though I be dead

1. None oth-er Lamb, none oth-er Name, None oth-er love's fire Thou art, how-e-ver cold I be: Nor heaven have I, nor Hope in heav'n or earth or sea, None oth-er hid-ing place to lay my head, Nor home but Thee. None be-side Thee.

2. My faith burns low, my hope burns low; On-ly my heart's de-sire cries out in me, By the deep thun-der place from guilt and shame, None be-side Thee. Cries out to Thee.

3. Lord, Thou art life, though I be dead; Love's fire Thou art, how-e-ver cold I be: Nor heav'n have I, nor place to lay my head, Nor home, but Thee. A - men.

by courtesy of United Reformed Church in England and Wales.

25 O the Deep, Deep

His Glory, Name, & Praise

... having loved his own ... he loved them to the end/Jn 13:1

S Trevor Francis (1834-1925)

Thomas J Williams (1869-1944)
Ton-y-botel   8 7 8 7 D

1. O the deep, deep love of Je - sus, Vast, un - mea - sured, bound - less, free; Rol - ling as a might - y o - cean In its full - ness o - ver me. Un - der - neath me, all a - round me, Is the cur - rent of Thy love; Lead - ing on - ward, lead - ing

2. O the deep, deep love of Je - sus, Spread His praise from shore to shore; How He lov - eth, e - ver lov - eth, Chang - eth ne - ver, ne - ver - more; How He watch - es o'er His loved ones, Died to call them all His own; How for them He in - ter -

3. O the deep, deep love of Je - sus, Love of e - v'ry love the best; 'Tis an o - cean vast of bles - sing, 'Tis a ha - ven sweet of rest, O the deep, deep love of Je - sus, 'Tis a Heav'n of Heav'ns to me; And it lifts me up to

home - ward, To my glo - rious rest a - bove.
ced - eth, Watch - eth o'er them from the throne.
glo - ry, For it lifts me up to Thee. A - men.

26 Fairest Lord Jesus

His Glory, Name, & Praise

You are the fairest of the sons of men/Ps 45:2

"Gesangbuch" Munster (1677)

Silesian Folk Melody
arr James Hopkirk
Crusaders' Hymn 5 6 8 5 5 8

1. Fair - est Lord Je - sus, Rul - er of all na - ture, O Thou of
2. Fair are the mea - dows, Fair - er still the wood-lands, Robed in the
3. Fair is the sun - shine, Fair - er still the moon-light, And fair the
4. All fair - est beau - ty, Hea - ven - ly and earth - ly, Won-drous - ly,

God and man the Son; Thee will I cher - ish, Thee will I
bloom - ing garb of spring; Je - sus is fair - er, Je - sus is
twink - ling star - ry host; Je - sus shines bright - er, Je - sus shines
Je - sus is found in Thee; None can be near - er, fair - er, or

hon - or Thou my soul's glo - ry, joy and crown.
pur - er, Who makes the woe - ful heart to sing.
pur - er, Than all the an - gels heav'n can boast.
dear - er, Than Thou my Sa - vior art to me. A - men.

music: © James Hopkirk.

27 Jesus, Thou Joy

... the hungry he fills with good things/Ps 107:9

Bernard of Clairvaux (c1150)
tr Ray Palmer (1808-1887)

Henry Baker (1835-1910)
Quebec 8 8 8 8

1. Je - sus, Thou Joy of lov - ing hearts, Thou Fount of life, Thou Light of men,
2. Thy truth un-changed hath e - ver stood; Thou sav - est those that on Thee call;
3. We taste Thee, O Thou liv - ing Bread, And long to feast up - on Thee still;
4. Our rest-less spi - rits yearn for Thee, Wher-e'er our change-ful lot is cast,
5. O Je - sus, e - ver with us stay, Make all our mo-ments calm and bright;

From the best bliss that earth im-parts We turn un-filled to Thee a - gain.
To them that seek Thee Thou art good, To them that find Thee All in all.
We drink of Thee, the Foun-tain-head, And thirst our souls from Thee to fill.
Glad when Thy gra-cious smile we see, Blest when our faith can hold Thee fast.
Chase the dark night of sin a - way, Shed o'er the world Thy ho - ly light. A - men.

28 Jesus, the Very Thought

Without having seen him you ... rejoice/1 Pet 1:8

Bernard of Clairvaux (c1150)
tr Edward Caswall (1814-1878)

John B Dykes (1823-1876)
St Agnes 8 6 8 6

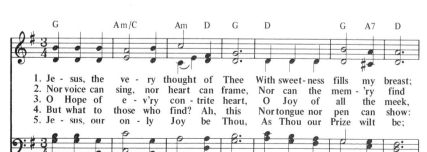

1. Je - sus, the ve - ry thought of Thee With sweet-ness fills my breast;
2. Nor voice can sing, nor heart can frame, Nor can the mem - 'ry find
3. O Hope of e - v'ry con - trite heart, O Joy of all the meek,
4. But what to those who find? Ah, this Nor tongue nor pen can show:
5. Je - sus, our on - ly Joy be Thou, As Thou our Prize wilt be;

But sweet - er far Thy face to see, And in Thy pres - ence rest.
A sweet - er sound than Thy blest Name, O Sa - vior of man - kind.
To those who fall, how kind Thou art! How good to those who seek.
The love of Je - sus, what it is None but His loved ones know.
Je - sus, be Thou our Glo - ry now, And through e - ter - ni - ty. A - men.

29 O Jesus, King

His Glory, Name, & Praise

I will extol thee, my God and King/Ps 145:1

Bernard of Clairvaux (c1150)
tr Edward Caswall (1814-1878)

Isaac Smith (1735-1800)
Abridge 8 6 8 6

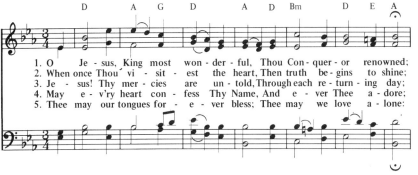

1. O Je - sus, King most won - der - ful, Thou Con - quer - or renowned;
2. When once Thou vi - sit - est the heart, Then truth be - gins to shine;
3. Je - sus! Thy mer - cies are un - told, Through each re - turn - ing day;
4. May e - v'ry heart con - fess Thy Name, And e - ver Thee a - dore;
5. Thee may our tongues for - e - ver bless; Thee may we love a - lone:

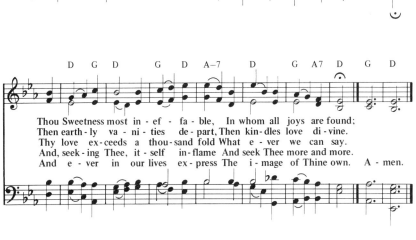

Thou Sweetness most in - ef - fa - ble, In whom all joys are found;
Then earth - ly va - ni - ties de - part, Then kin - dles love di - vine.
Thy love ex - ceeds a thou - sand fold What e - ver we can say.
And, seek - ing Thee, it - self in - flame And seek Thee more and more.
And e - ver in our lives ex - press The i - mage of Thine own. A - men.

30 Thine Be the Glory

His Glory, Name, & Praise

. . . God, who gives us the victory through our Lord Jesus Christ/1 Cor 15:57

Edmond Budry (1854-1932)
tr Richard B Hoyle (1875-1939)

"Judas Maccabaeus"
George F Handel (1685-1759)
Maccabaeus 10 11 11 11 w/refrain

1. Thine be the glory, ris - en, con - qu'ring Son,
2. Lo! Je - sus meets us, ris - en from the tomb;
3. No more we doubt Thee, glo - rious Prince of life;

End - less is the vic - t'ry Thou o'er death hast won;
Lov - ing - ly He greets us, scat - ters fear and gloom;
Life is nought with - out Thee: aid us in our strife;

An - gels in bright rai - ment rolled the stone a - way,
Let the Church with glad - ness, hymns of tri - umph sing,
Make us more than con - qu'rors, thro' Thy death - less love:

Kept the fold - ed grave - clothes, where Thy bod - y lay.
For her Lord now liv - eth, death hath lost its sting.
Bring us safe thro' Jor - dan to Thy home a - bove.

Refrain

Thine be the glo-ry, ris-en, con-qu'ring Son, End-less is the
vic - t'ry Thou o'er death hast won. A - men.

words: © *World Student Federation. Used by permission.*

31   O for a Thousand Tongues   His Glory, Name, & Praise

Then my tongue shall tell of thy ... praise all the day long/Ps 35:28

Charles Wesley (1707-1788)

Carl Gläser (1784-1829)
arr Lowell Mason (1792-1872)
Azmon 8 6 8 6

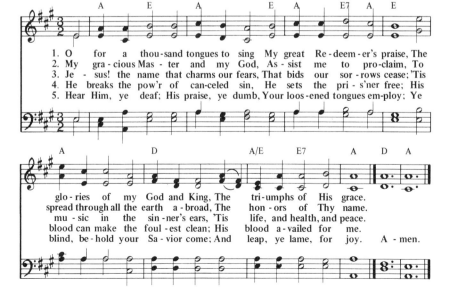

1. O   for a thou-sand tongues to sing My great Re-deem-er's praise, The
2. My gra-cious Mas-ter and my God, As-sist me to pro-claim, To
3. Je - sus! the name that charms our fears, That bids our sor-rows cease; 'Tis
4. He breaks the pow'r of can-celed sin, He sets the pri-s'ner free; His
5. Hear Him, ye deaf; His praise, ye dumb, Your loos-ened tongues em-ploy; Ye

glo-ries of my God and King, The tri-umphs of His grace.
spread through all the earth a-broad, The hon-ors of Thy name.
mu - sic in the sin-ner's ears, 'Tis life, and health, and peace.
blood can make the foul-est clean; His blood a-vailed for me.
blind, be-hold your Sa-vior come; And leap, ye lame, for joy. A - men.

32 O for a Thousand Tongues — His Glory, Name, & Praise

Then my tongue shall tell of thy... praise all the day long/Ps 35:28

Charles Wesley (1707-1788)

Hughes M Huffman (1942-   )
Deborah 8 6 8 6 D

1. O for a thou-sand tongues to sing My great Re-deem-er's praise,
2. My gra-cious Mas-ter and my God, As-sist me to pro-claim,
3. He speaks, and list-'ning to his voice, New life the dead re-ceive,

The glo-ries of my God and King, The tri-umphs of his grace!
To spread through all the earth a-broad The hon-ors of Thy Name.
The mourn-ful bro-ken hearts re-joice, The hum-ble poor be-lieve.

Je-sus the Name that charms our fears, That bids our sor-rows cease,
He breaks the pow'r of can-celed sin, He sets the pris-'ner free;
Hear him, ye deaf; His praise, ye dumb, Your loos-ened tongues em-ploy;

'Tis mu-sic in the sin-ner's ears,'Tis life and health and peace.
His Blood can make the foul-est clean,His Blood a-vailed for me.
Ye blind, be-hold your Sa-vior come;And leap, ye lame, for joy. A-men.

33 All Hail the Power

His Glory, Name, & Praise

... he has a name inscribed, King of kings and Lord of lords/Rev 19:16

Edward Perronet (1726-1792)
stanza 4 John Rippon (1751-1836)

James Ellor (1819-1899)
Diadem 8 6 8 6 w/refrain

1. All hail the pow'r of Je - sus' name! Let an - gels pros - trate
2. Ye cho - sen seed of Is - rael's race; Ye ran - somed from the
3. Sin - ners, whose love can ne'er for - get The worm-wood and the
4. Let e - v'ry kin - dred, e - v'ry tribe, On this ter - res - trial
5. O that with yon - der sa - cred throng We at His feet may

fall, Let an - gels pros - trate fall; Bring forth the ro - yal
fall, Ye ran - somed from the fall; Hail Him who saves you
gall, The worm - wood and the gall, Go, spread your tro - phies
ball, On this ter - res - trial ball, To Him all ma - jes -
fall, We at His feet may fall! We'll join the e - ver -

(refrain)

di - a - dem,
by His grace,
at His feet, And crown   Him,
ty as - cribe,
last - ing song,   crown Him,   crown Him,   crown Him,   crown Him

crown

crown Him,   crown Him,   crown Him, And crown Him Lord of   all.   A - men.

Him.

34 All Glory, Laud and Honor   His Glory, Name, & Praise

Rejoice greatly . . . Lo, your king comes to you/Zech 9:9

Theodulph of Orleans (c 760-821)
tr John M Neale (1818-1866)

Melchoir Teschner (1584-1635)
St Theodulph 7 6 7 6 D

All glo - ry, laud and hon - or to Thee, Re - deem - er, King,

To whom the lips of chil - dren made sweet ho - san - nas ring!   *Fine*

1. Thou art the King of Is - rael, Thou Da - vid's ro - yal Son,
2. The com - pan - y of an - gels are prais - ing Thee on high,
3. The peo - ple of the He - brews with palms be - fore Thee went,
4. To Thee be - fore Thy pas - sion they sang their hymns of praise;
5. Thou didst ac - cept their prais - es; ac - cept the prayers we bring;

D.C. al Fine

Who in the Lord's name com - est, the King and bles - sed one.
And mor - tal men and all things cre - a - ted make re - ply.
Our praise and prayer and an - thems be - fore Thee we pre - sent.
To Thee now high ex - al - ted our me - lo - dy we raise.
Who in all good de - light - est, Thou good and gra - cious King.

35 God of Gods

His Glory, Name, & Praise

Praise the LORD from the heavens/Ps 148:1

Timothy Dudley-Smith

Christian Strover
8 7 8 7 8 8 8 7

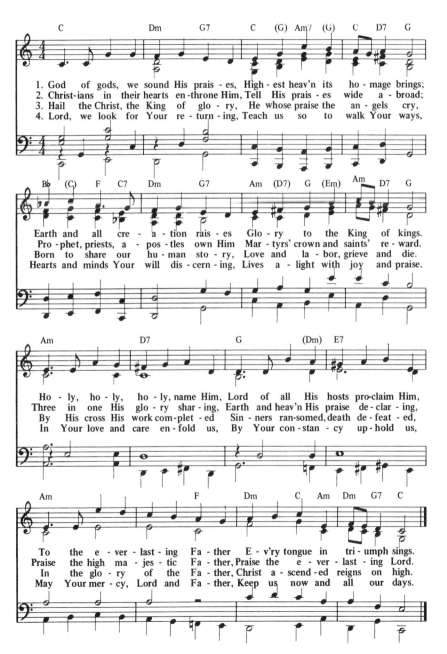

1. God of gods, we sound His prais-es, High-est heav'n its ho-mage brings;
2. Christ-ians in their hearts en-throne Him, Tell His prais-es wide a-broad;
3. Hail the Christ, the King of glo-ry, He whose praise the an-gels cry,
4. Lord, we look for Your re-turn-ing, Teach us so to walk Your ways,

Earth and all cre-a-tion rais-es Glo-ry to the King of kings.
Pro-phet, priests, a-pos-tles own Him Mar-tyrs' crown and saints' re-ward.
Born to share our hu-man sto-ry, Love and la-bor, grieve and die.
Hearts and minds Your will dis-cern-ing, Lives a-light with joy and praise.

Ho-ly, ho-ly, ho-ly, name Him, Lord of all His hosts pro-claim Him,
Three in one His glo-ry shar-ing, Earth and heav'n His praise de-clar-ing,
By His cross His work com-plet-ed Sin-ners ran-somed, death de-feat-ed,
In Your love and care en-fold us, By Your con-stan-cy up-hold us,

To the e-ver-last-ing Fa-ther E-v'ry tongue in tri-umph sings.
Praise the high ma-jes-tic Fa-ther, Praise the e-ver-last-ing Lord.
In the glo-ry of the Fa-ther, Christ a-scend-ed reigns on high.
May Your mer-cy, Lord and Fa-ther, Keep us now and all our days.

36 All Is in Christ

His Glory, Name, & Praise

... his purpose ... set forth in Christ ... to unite all things in him/Eph 1:10

Claire-Lise de Benoit (1917-   )
tr Lois Thiessen

J S Bach (1685-1750)
11 8 7 8 7 8 8 7 7

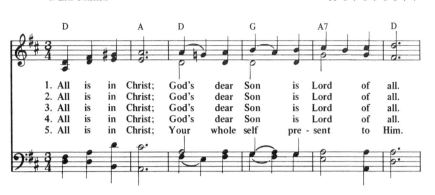

1. All is in Christ; God's dear Son is Lord of all.
2. All is in Christ; God's dear Son is Lord of all.
3. All is in Christ; God's dear Son is Lord of all.
4. All is in Christ; God's dear Son is Lord of all.
5. All is in Christ; Your whole self pre - sent to Him.

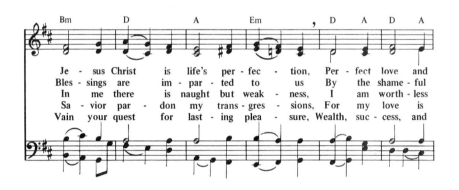

Je - sus Christ is life's per - fec - tion, Per - fect love and
Bles - sings are im - par - ted to us By the shame - ful
In me there is naught but weak - ness, I am worth - less
Sa - vior par - don my trans - gres - sions, For my love is
Vain your quest for last - ing plea - sure, Wealth, suc - cess, and

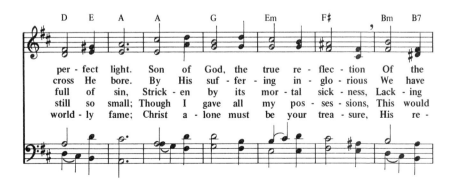

per - fect light. Son of God, the true re - flec - tion Of the
cross He bore. By His suf - fer - ing in - glo - rious We have
full of sin, Strick - en by its mor - tal sick - ness, Lack - ing
still so small; Though I gave all my pos - ses - sions, This would
world - ly fame; Christ a - lone must be your trea - sure, His re -

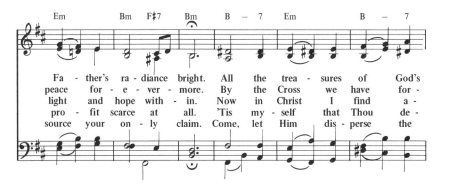

Fa - ther's ra - diance bright. All the trea - sures of God's
peace for - e - ver - more. By the Cross we have for -
light and hope with - in. Now in Christ I find a -
source your on - ly claim. Come, let Him dis - perse the

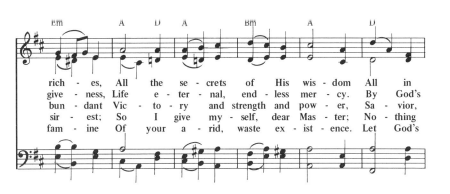

rich - es, All the se - crets of His wis - dom All in
give - ness, Life e - ter - nal, end - less mer - cy. By God's
bun - dant Vic - to - ry and strength and pow - er, Sa - vior,
sir - est; So I give my - self, dear Mas - ter; No - thing
fam - ine Of your a - rid, waste ex - ist - ence. Let God's

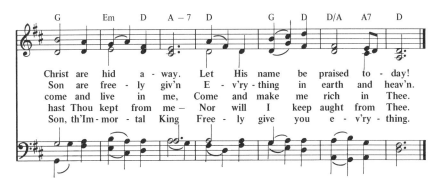

Christ are hid a - way. Let His name be praised to - day!
Son are free - ly giv'n E - v'ry - thing in earth and heav'n.
come and live in me, Come and make me rich in Thee.
hast Thou kept from me — Nor will I keep aught from Thee.
Son, th'Im - mor - tal King Free - ly give you e - v'ry - thing.

37 Crown Him with Many

His Glory, Name, & Praise

... and on his head are many diadems/Rev 19:12

Matthew Bridges (1800-1894)
stanza 2 Godfrey Thring (1823-1903)

George Elvey (1816-1893)
Diademata 6 6 8 6 D

1. Crown Him with man - y crowns, The Lamb up - on His throne;
2. Crown Him the Lord of life, Who tri - umphed o'er the grave,
3. Crown Him the Lord of peace, Whose pow'r a scep - ter sways
4. Crown Him the Lord of love; Be - hold His hands and side,

Hark! how the heav'n - ly an - them drowns All mu - sic but its own.
And rose vic - to - rious in the strife For those He came to save;
From pole to pole that wars may cease, And all be prayer and praise;
Those wounds yet vi - si - ble a - bove, In beau - ty glo - ri - fied:

A - wake, my soul, and sing Of Him who died for thee,
His glo - ries now we sing, Who died and rose on high,
His reign shall know no end, And round His pier - ced feet
All hail, Re - deem - er, hail! For Thou hast died for me:

And hail Him as thy match - less King Through all e - ter - ni - ty.
Who died e - ter - nal life to bring, And lives, that death may die.
Fair flowers of par - a - dise ex - tend Their fra - grance e - ver sweet.
Thy praise and glo - ry shall not fail Through - out e - ter - ni - ty. A-men.

... he humbled himself and became obedient unto death/Phil 2:8

American Folk Hymn

"Southern Harmony" (1835)
arr Hughes M Huffman (1942-   )
Wondrous Love   12 9 6 6 12 9

1. What won-drous love is this, O my soul, O my soul! What won-drous love is this, O my soul! What won-drous love is this That caused the Lord of bliss To bear the dread-ful curse for my soul, for my soul, To bear the dread-ful curse for my soul.

2. When I was sink-ing down, sink-ing down, sink-ing down, When I was sink-ing down, sink-ing down, When I was sink-ing down Be-neath God's right-eous frown, Christ laid a-side his crown for my soul, for my soul, Christ laid a-side his crown for my soul.

3. To God and to the Lamb I will sing, I will sing, To God and to the Lamb I will sing, To God and to the Lamb who is the great "I AM," while mil-lions join the theme, I will sing, I will sing, While mil-lions join the theme, I will sing.

4. And when from death I'm free, I'll sing on, I'll sing on, And when from death I'm free I'll sing on, And when from death I'm free, I'll sing and joy-ful be, And through e-ter-ni-ty I'll sing on, I'll sing on, And through e-ter-ni-ty I'll sing on.

39 Tell Out My Soul

"My soul magnifies the Lord"/Lk 1:46

Timothy Dudley-Smith

Walter Greatorex (1877-1949)
Woodlands 10 10 10 10

1. Tell out, my soul, the great-ness of the Lord! Un-num-ber'd bles-sings, give my spi-rit voice; Ten-der to me the pro-mise of His word; In God my Sa-vior shall my heart re-joice.

2. Tell out, my soul, the great-ness of His Name! Make known His might, the deeds His arm has done; His mer-cy sure, from age to age the same; His Ho-ly Name— the Lord, the Might-y One.

3. Tell out, my soul, the great-ness of His might! Pow'rs and do-mi-nions lay their glo-ry by. Proud hearts and stub-born wills are put to flight, The hun-gry fed, the hum-ble lift-ed high.

4. Tell out, my soul, the glo-ries of His word! Firm is His pro-mise, and His mer-cy sure. Tell out, my soul, the great-ness of the Lord To chil-dren's chil-dren and for e-ver-more!

40 My Soul Proclaims

His Glory, Name, & Praise

"My soul magnifies the Lord"/Lk 1:46

Christopher Idle (1938-   )

Norman Warren (1934-   )
10 12 10 13 9

1. My soul proclaims the greatness of the Lord And my spirit sings for joy to my Savior God! His lowly slave He looked upon in love; They will call me happy now, for mighty are the works He has done and holy is His Name!

2. In ev'ry age, for those who fear the Lord Comes His mercy, and the strength of His mighty arm; He routs the proud, throws monarchs off their thrones, While He lifts the lowly high, fills hungry men with food, And the rich sends empty away.

3. To Israel His servant He brings help And the promise to our fathers is now fulfilled; For Christ has come according to His word, And the mercy that He showed to Abraham is now For His children's children evermore.

41 O Listen

... tell of all his wonderful works!/Ps 105:2

William Owen (1814-1893)
alt James M Gray (1851-1935)

William Owen (1814-1893)
What Did He Do? 9 7 9 7 w/refrain

1. O lis - ten to our won - drous sto - ry Count - ed
2. No an - gel could His place have tak - en, High - est
3. Will you sur - ren - der to this Sa - vior? To His

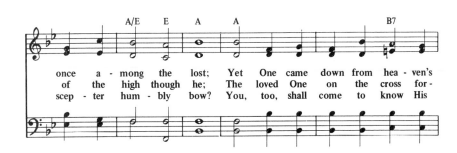

once a - mong the lost; Yet One came down from hea - ven's
of the high though he; The loved One on the cross for -
scep - ter hum - bly bow? You, too, shall come to know His

Chorus

glo - ry Sav - ing us at aw - ful cost!
sak - en Was One of the God - head three! Who
fa - vor, He will save you, save you now.

saved us from e - ter - nal loss?
Who but God's Son up -

What did He do? Where is He now?
on the cross? He died for you! Be -

In hea - ven in - ter - ced - ing!
lieve it thou, In hea - ven in - ter - ced - ing!

42 "Man of Sorrows"   His Glory, Name, & Praise

He was despised and rejected by men; a man of sorrows/Is 53:3

Philip Bliss (1838-1876)

Philip Bliss (1838-1876)
Man of Sorrows   7 7 7 8

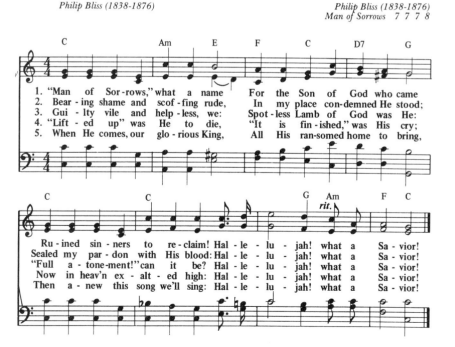

1. "Man of Sor - rows," what a name   For the Son of God who came
2. Bear - ing shame and scof - fing rude,   In my place con - demned He stood;
3. Gui - lty vile and help - less, we: Spot - less Lamb of God was He:
4. "Lift - ed up" was He to die,   "It is fin - ished," was His cry;
5. When He comes, our glo - rious King,   All His ran - somed home to bring,

Ru - ined sin - ners to re - claim! Hal - le - lu - jah! what a Sa - vior!
Sealed my par - don with His blood: Hal - le - lu - jah! what a Sa - vior!
"Full a - tone - ment!" can it be? Hal - le - lu - jah! what a Sa - vior!
Now in heav'n ex - alt - ed high: Hal - le - lu - jah! what a Sa - vior!
Then a - new this song we'll sing: Hal - le - lu - jah! what a Sa - vior!

43 Lamb of God!

His Glory, Name, & Praise

Worthy is the Lamb ... to receive ... honor and glory and blessing/Rev 5:12

James G Deck (1802-1884)

James Langran (1835-1909)
Deerhurst 8 7 8 7 D

1. Lamb of God! Our souls adore Thee, While upon Thy face we gaze; There the Father's love and glory Shine in all their brightest rays; Thine Almighty pow'r and wisdom All creation's works proclaim;

2. Lamb of God! Thy Father's bosom Ever was Thy dwelling place; His delight, in Him rejoicing, One with Him in pow'r and grace; Oh, what wondrous love and mercy! Thou didst lay Thy glory by;

3. Lamb of God! When we behold Thee Lowly in the manger laid, Wand'ring as a homeless stranger, For our guilt and folly stricken, In the world Thy hands had made; When we see Thee in the garden In Thine agony of blood;

4. When we see Thee, as the victim, Bound to the accursed tree, For our guilt and folly stricken, All our judgment borne by Thee, Lord, we own, with hearts adoring, Thou hast loved us unto blood;

5. Lamb of God! Thou soon in glory Wilt to this sad earth return; All Thy foes shall quake before Thee, All that now despise Thee mourn; Then Thy saints all gather'd to Thee, With Thee in Thy kingdom reign;

Heav'n and earth a - like con - fess Thee As the e - ver great "I AM."
And for us didst come from hea - ven As the Lamb of God to die.
At Thy grace we are con - found - ed, Ho - ly, Spot - less, Lamb of God!
Glo - ry, glo - ry e - ver - last - ing Be to Thee, Thou Lamb of God.
Thine the praise and Thine the glo - ry, Lamb of God, for sin - ners slain!

44 How Sweet the Name

His Glory, Name, & Praise

To you therefore who believe, he is precious/1 Pet 2:7

John Newton (1725-1807)

Cuthbert Howard (1856-1927)
Lloyd 8 6 8 6

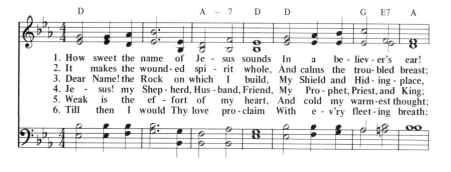

1. How sweet the name of Je - sus sounds In a be - liev - er's ear!
2. It makes the wound - ed spi - rit whole, And calms the trou - bled breast;
3. Dear Name! the Rock on which I build, My Shield and Hid - ing - place,
4. Je - sus! my Shep - herd, Hus - band, Friend, My Pro - phet, Priest, and King;
5. Weak is the ef - fort of my heart, And cold my warm - est thought;
6. Till then I would Thy love pro - claim With e - v'ry fleet - ing breath;

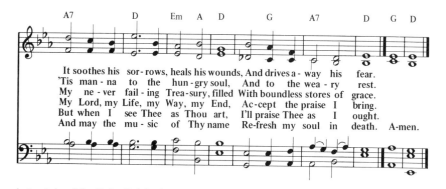

It soothes his sor - rows, heals his wounds, And drives a - way his fear.
'Tis man - na to the hun - gry soul, And to the wea - ry rest.
My ne - ver fail - ing Trea - sury, filled With boundless stores of grace.
My Lord, my Life, my Way, my End, Ac - cept the praise I bring.
But when I see Thee as Thou art, I'll praise Thee as I ought.
And may the mu - sic of Thy name Re - fresh my soul in death. A - men.

by permission of Geo Taylor, Stainland, Halifax, England.

45 Jesus! the Name

His Glory, Name, & Praise

God has ... bestowed on him the name which is above every name/Phil 2:9

Charles Wesley (1707-1788)

Thomas Phillips (1735-1807)
Lydia   8 6 8 6

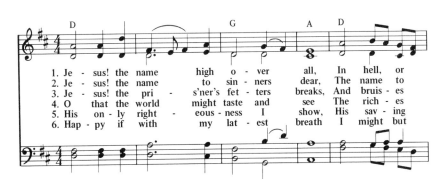

1. Je - sus! the name high o - ver all, In hell, or
2. Je - sus! the name to sin - ners dear, The name to
3. Je - sus! the pri - s'ner's fet - ters breaks, And bruis - es
4. O that the world might taste and see The rich - es
5. His on - ly right - eous - ness I show, His sav - ing
6. Hap - py if with my lat - est breath I might but

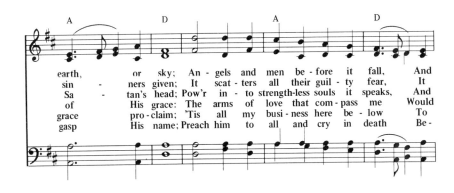

earth, or sky; An - gels and men be - fore it fall, And
sin - ners given; It scat - ters all their guil - ty fear, It
Sa - tan's head; Pow'r in - to strength-less souls it speaks, And
of His grace: The arms of love that com - pass me Would
grace pro - claim; 'Tis all my busi - ness here be - low To
gasp His name; Preach him to all and cry in death Be -

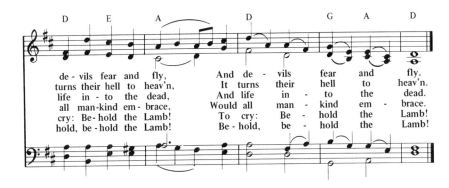

de - vils fear and fly, And de - vils fear and fly.
turns their hell to heav'n, It turns their hell to the heav'n.
life in - to the dead, And life in - to the dead.
all man-kind em - brace, Would all man - kind em - brace.
cry: Be- hold the Lamb! To cry: Be - hold the Lamb!
hold, be - hold the Lamb! Be - hold, be - hold the Lamb!

46 When Morning Gilds

His Glory, Name, & Praise

O LORD, in the morning thou dost hear my voice/Ps 5:3

"Katholisches Gesangbuch" Würzburg (1828)
tr Edward Caswall (1814-1878)

Joseph Barnby (1838-1896)
Laudes Domini 6 6 6 6 6 6

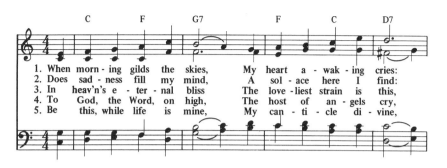

1. When morn - ing gilds the skies, My heart a - wak - ing cries:
2. Does sad - ness fill my mind, A sol - ace here I find:
3. In heav'n's e - ter - nal bliss The love - liest strain is this,
4. To God, the Word, on high, The host of an - gels cry,
5. Be this, while life is mine, My can - ti - cle di - vine,

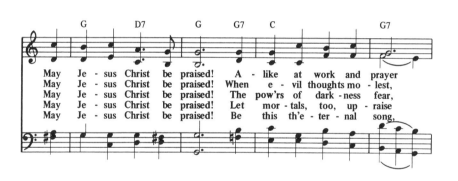

May Je - sus Christ be praised! A - like at work and prayer
May Je - sus Christ be praised! When e - vil thoughts mo - lest,
May Je - sus Christ be praised! The pow'rs of dark - ness fear,
May Je - sus Christ be praised! Let mor - tals, too, up - raise
May Je - sus Christ be praised! Be this th'e - ter - nal song,

To Je - sus I re - pair: May Je - sus Christ be praised!
With this I shield my breast— May Je - sus Christ be praised!
When this sweet chant they hear: May Je - sus Christ be praised!
Their voice in hymns of praise; May Je - sus Christ be praised!
Through all the a - ges long: May Je - sus Christ be praised! A - men.

God the Son: *His life and work*

Thou who wast rich beyond all splendor,
All for love's sake becamest poor;
Thrones for a manger didst surrender,
Sapphire paved courts for stable floor.
Thou who wast rich beyond all splendor,
All for love's sake becamest poor.

Frank Houghton

47 O Come, O Come Emmanuel His Life & Work

... and they will see the Son of man coming on the clouds/Mt 24:30

"Great O Antiphons" (12th-13th centuries) *French Missal*
tr John M Neale (1818-1866) *adpt Thomas Helmore (1811-1890)*
Veni Immanuel 8 8 8 8 8 8

1. O come, O come Em - ma - nu - el, And ran - som cap - tive
2. O come, O come, Thou Lord of might Who to Thy tribes, on
3. O come, Thou Rod of Jes - se, free Thine own from Sa - tan's
4. O come, Thou Day - spring, come and cheer Our spi - rits by Thine
5. O come, Thou Key of Da - vid, come And o - pen wide our

I - sra - el, That mourns in low - ly e - xile here,
Si - nai's height, In an - cient times did give the law
ty - ran - ny; From depths of hell Thy peo - ple save,
ad - vent here; Dis - perse the gloom - y clouds of night,
hea - v'nly home; Make safe the way that leads on high,

Un - til the Son of God ap - pear,
In cloud and ma - jes - ty and awe:
And give them vic - t'ry o'er the grave: Re - joice, re - joice! Em -
And death's dark sha - dows put to flight:
And close the path to mi - se - ry:

ma - nu - el Shall come to thee, O I - sra - el. A - men.

48 From Jesse's Stock Up-Springing

There shall come forth a shoot from the stump of Jesse/Is 11:1

German Carol
tr Mary E Butler (1841-1916)

German Melody
Es Ist Ein' Ros Entsprungen   7 6 7 6 6 6 7 6

1. From Jes - se's stock up - spring - ing, On ten - der root has grown:
2. This rose then of my sto - ry I - sai - ah did pro - claim.
3. The rose - bud small and ten - der Gives fra - grance e - v'ry day.

A rose by Pro - phet's sing - ing To all the world made known.
What God or - dained in glo - ry, By bles - sed Ma - ry came.
And by its bril - liant splen - dor Makes dark - ness pass a - way.

The rose 'midst win - ter's cold, A love - ly blos - som
The Child the Vir - gin bore, The world's sal - va - tion
True God, true Man we pray, Help us in e - v'ry

bear - ing, In form - er days fore - told.
bring - ing Through Him for e - ver - more.
sor - row, And guard us on our way. A - men.

Thou Who Wast Rich   His Life & Work

. . . though he was rich, yet for your sake he became poor/2 Cor 8:9

Frank Houghton (1894-1972)

French Carol Melody
arr Charles H Kitson (1874-1944)
Fragrance 9 8 9 8 9 8

1. Thou who wast rich be-yond all splen-dor, All for love's sake be-
2. Thou who art God be-yond all prais-ing, All for love's sake be-
3. Thou who art love be-yond all tel-ling, Sa-vior and King, we

cam-est poor; Thrones for a man-ger didst sur-ren-der,
cam-est Man; Stoop-ing so low, but sin-ners rais-ing
wor-ship Thee. Em-ma-nu-el, with-in us dwel-ling

Sap-phire paved courts for sta-ble floor. Thou who wast rich be-
Heav'n-ward by Thine e-ter-nal plan. Thou who art God be-
Make us what Thou wouldst have us be. Thou who art love, be-

yond all splen-dor, All for love's sake be-cam-est poor.
yond all prais-ing, All for love's sake be-cam-est Man.
yond all tel-ling, Sa-vior and King, we wor-ship Thee.

50 Cradled in a Manger, Meanly

His Life & Work

... there was no place for them in the inn/Lk 2:7

George S Rowe (1830-1913)

Plymouth Collection (1855)
Pleading Savior 8 7 8 7 D

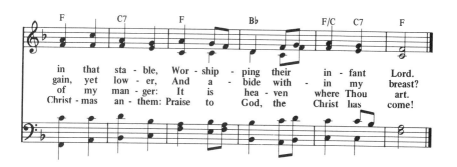

in that sta - ble, Wor - ship - ping their in - fant Lord.
gain, yet low - er, And a - bide with - in my breast?
of my man - ger: It is hea - ven where Thou art.
Christ - mas an - them: Praise to God, the Christ has come!

51 Child in the Manger

His Life & Work

Therefore God has highly exalted him/Phil 2:9

Mary MacDonald (1817-c1890)
tr Lachlan MacBean (1853-1931)

Gaelic Melody
Bunessan 5 5 5 3 D

1. Child in the man - ger, In - fant of Ma - ry;
   Out - cast and
2. Once the most ho - ly Child of sal - va - tion
   Gent - ly and
3. Pro - phets fore - told him In - fant of won - der;
   An - gels be -

stran - ger, Lord of all; Child who in - her - its All our trans-
low - ly Lived be - low; Now as our glo - rious Might - y Re-
hold him On his throne; Wor - thy our Sa - vior Of all our

gres - sions, All our de - me - rits On him fall.
deem - er, See him vic - to - rious O'er each foe.
prais - es; Hap - py for - e - ver Are his own.

52　Once in Royal David's City

His Life & Work

And the Word became flesh and dwelt among us/Jn 1:14

Cecil F Alexander (1818-1895)

Henry J Gauntlett (1805-1876)
Irby　8 7 8 7 7 7

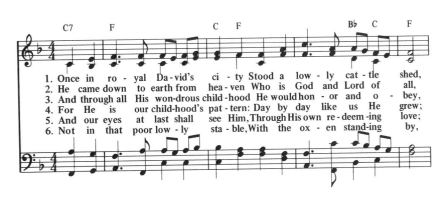

1. Once in ro - yal Da-vid's ci - ty Stood a low - ly cat - tle shed,
2. He came down to earth from hea - ven Who is God and Lord of all,
3. And through all His won-drous child-hood He would hon - or and o - bey,
4. For He is our child-hood's pat - tern: Day by day like us He grew;
5. And our eyes at last shall see Him, Through His own re-deem-ing love;
6. Not in that poor low - ly sta - ble, With the ox - en stand-ing by,

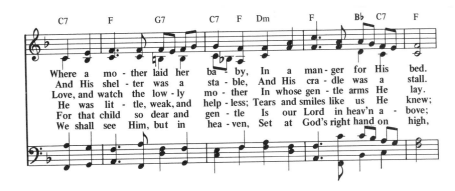

Where a mo - ther laid her ba - by, In a man - ger for His bed.
And His shel - ter was a sta - ble, And His cra - dle was a stall.
Love, and watch the low - ly mo - ther In whose gen - tle arms He lay.
He was lit - tle, weak, and help - less; Tears and smiles like us He knew;
For that child so dear and gen - tle Is our Lord in heav'n a - bove,
We shall see Him, but in hea - ven, Set at God's right hand on high,

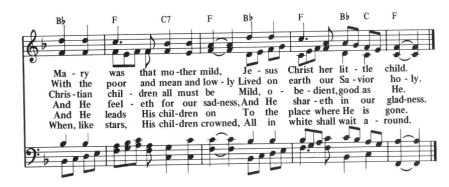

Ma - ry was that mo-ther mild, Je - sus Christ her lit - tle child.
With the poor and mean and low - ly Lived on earth our Sa - vior ho - ly.
Chris - tian chil - dren all must be Mild, o - be - dient, good as He.
And He feel - eth for our sad-ness, And He shar - eth in our glad-ness.
And He leads His chil-dren on To the place where He is gone.
When, like stars, His chil-dren crowned, All in white shall wait a - round.

53 Sing Lullaby!

His Life & Work

... they saw the child ... and they fell down and worshipped him/Mt 2:11

Sabine Baring-Gould (1834-1924)

Old Basque Noel
arr Charles E Pettiman (1866-1943)
Infant King 4 9 4 8 9 9 4

1. Sing lul-la-by! Lul-la-by ba-by, now re-clin-ing
2. Sing lul-la-by! Lul-la-by ba-by, now a-sleep-ing,
3. Sing lul-la-by! Lul-la-by ba-by, now a-doz-ing,
4. Sing lul-la-by! Lul-la-by! is the babe a-wak-ing?

Sing lul-la-by! Hush, do not wake the In-fant King.
Sing lul-la-by! Hush, do not wake the In-fant King.
Sing lul-la-by! Hush, do not wake the In-fant King.
Sing lul-la-by! Hush, do not stir the In-fant King.

An-gels are watch-ing, stars are shin-ing O-ver the
Soon will come sor-row with the morn-ing, Soon will come
Soon comes the cross, the nails, the pierc-ing, Then in the
Dream-ing of Ea-ster, glad-some morn-ing. Con-quer-ing

place where He is ly-ing: Sing lul-la-by.
bit-ter grief and weep-ing: Sing lul-la-by.
grave at last re-pos-ing: Sing lul-la-by.
Death, its bond-age break-ing:

54 Of the Father's Love Begotten

His Life & Work

In the beginning was the Word . . . and the Word was God/Jn 1:1

Aurelius C Prudentius (4th century)
tr John M Neale (1818-1866)
tr Henry W Baker (1821-1877)

Medieval Melody "Piae Cantiones" (1582)
arr Winfred Douglas (1867-1944)
Divinum Mysterium 8 7 8 7 8 7 7

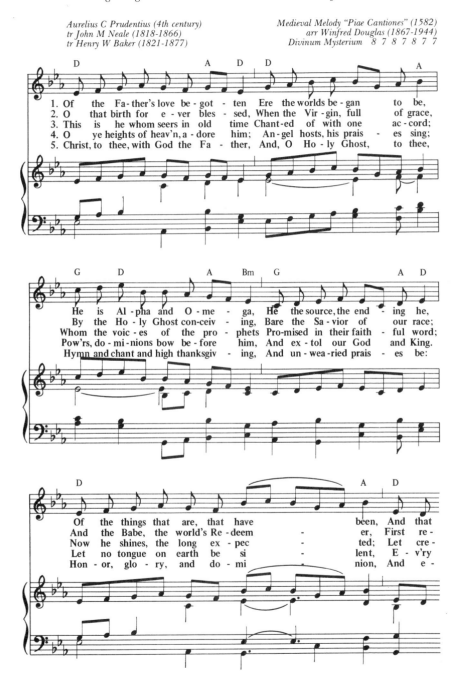

1. Of the Fa-ther's love be-got - ten Ere the worlds be-gan to be,
2. O that birth for e - ver bles - sed, When the Vir-gin, full of grace,
3. This is he whom seers in old time Chant-ed of with one ac - cord;
4. O ye heights of heav'n, a - dore him; An-gel hosts, his prais - es sing;
5. Christ, to thee, with God the Fa - ther, And, O Ho-ly Ghost, to thee,

He is Al-pha and O - me - ga, He the source, the end - ing he,
By the Ho - ly Ghost con-ceiv - ing, Bare the Sa - vior of our race;
Whom the voic - es of the pro - phets Pro-mised in their faith - ful word;
Pow'rs, do - mi-nions bow be - fore him, And ex - tol our God and King.
Hymn and chant and high thanksgiv - ing, And un - wea-ried prais - es be:

Of the things that are, that have been, And that
And the Babe, the world's Re - deem - er, First
Now he shines, the long ex - pec - ted; Let cre -
Let no tongue on earth be si - lent, E - v'ry
Hon - or, glo - ry, and do - mi - nion, And e -

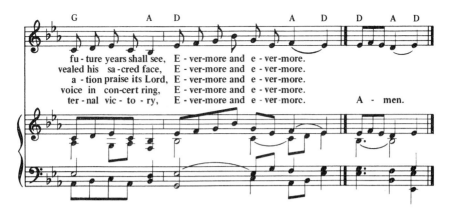

fu - ture years shall see, E - ver-more and e - ver-more.
vealed his sa - cred face, E - ver-more and e - ver-more.
a - tion praise its Lord, E - ver-more and e - ver-more.
voice in con-cert ring, E - ver-more and e - ver-more.
ter - nal vic - to - ry, E - ver-more and e - ver-more. A - men.

55 The Darkness Turns to Dawn His Life & Work

For to us a child is born, to us a son is given/Is 9.6

Timothy Dudley-Smith

Norman Warren (1934-   )
6 6 8 6

1. The dark-ness turns to dawn, The day-spring shines from heav'n,
2. The Son of God most high, Be - fore all else be - gan,
3. God's Word of truth and grace Made flesh with us to dwell;
4. How rich His heav'n - ly home! How poor His hu - man birth!
5. A ser - vant's form, a slave, The Lord con-sents to share;
6. O - be - dient and a - lone Up - on that cross to die —
7. And still God sheds a - broad That love so strong to send

For un - to us a child is born, To us a Son is giv'n.
A vir - gin's son be - hold Him lie, The new-born Son of Man.
The bright-ness of the Fa - ther's face, The child Em - ma - nu - el.
As mor - tal man He stoops to come, The light and life of earth.
Our sin and shame, our cross and grave, He bows Him-self to bear.
And then to share the Fa - ther's throne In ma - jes - ty on high.
A Sa - vior, who is Christ the Lord, Whose reign shall ne - ver end.

56 O Leave Your Sheep

His Life & Work

...for to you is born this day... a Savior/Lk 2:11

French Carol
tr Alice Raleigh (1857-1941)

French Carol Melody
arr Marjorie T Renton (1901-   )
Quittez Pasteurs   11 10 11 6 12

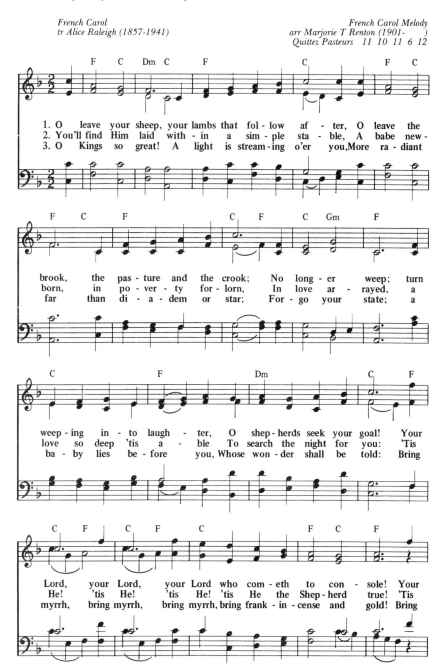

1. O leave your sheep, your lambs that fol-low af - ter, O leave the
2. You'll find Him laid with-in a sim-ple sta - ble, A babe new-
3. O Kings so great! A light is stream-ing o'er you, More ra - diant

brook, the pas-ture and the crook; No long-er weep; turn
born, in po-ver-ty for-lorn, In love ar - rayed, a
far than di - a - dem or star; For - go your state; a

weep-ing in - to laugh - ter, O shep-herds seek your goal! Your
love so deep 'tis a - ble To search the night for you: 'Tis
ba - by lies be - fore you, Whose won - der shall be told: Bring

Lord, your Lord, your Lord who com - eth to con - sole! Your
He! 'tis He! 'tis He! 'tis He the Shep-herd true! 'Tis
myrrh, bring myrrh, bring myrrh, bring frank - in - cense and gold! Bring

C   F   C   F   B♭   F/C   C7   F

Lord,   your   Lord,   your   Lord who com - eth   to   con - sole!
He!   'tis   He!   'tis   He! 'tis He the   Shep - herd   true!
myrrh,   bring myrrh,   bring   myrrh, bring frank - in - cense and   gold!

57   Complete in Thee!   His Life & Work

... and you have come to fulness of life in him/Col 2:10

Cecil F Alexander (1823-1895)   William Smallwood (1831-1897)
Antwerp   8 8 8 8

D   Bm   A7   D   A

1. Com - plete in Thee! no work of mine   May take, dear
2. Com - plete in Thee! no more shall sin,   Thy grace hath
3. Com - plete in Thee! each want sup - plied,   And no good
4. Dear Sa - vior! when be - fore thy bar   All tribes and

D   E   E7   A   D   G   Em   B

Lord, the place of Thine;   Thy blood hath par - don bought for
con - quered, reign with - in;   Thy voice shall bid the temp - ter
thing to me de - nied;   Since Thou my por - tion, Lord, wilt
tongues as - sem - bled are,   A - mong Thy cho - sen will I

Em   A   Bm   G   A7   D   G   D

me, And I am now com - plete in Thee.
flee. And I shall stand com - plete in Thee.
be, I ask no more, com - plete in Thee.
be, At Thy right hand com - plete in Thee. A - men.

But when the time had fully come, God sent forth his Son/Gal 4:4

William Y Fullerton (1857-1932)

Traditional Irish Melody
arr Marc Hedlin (1942-　　)
Londonderry Air　11 10 11 10 D

1. I can-not tell why He whom an - gels wor - ship Should set His
2. I can-not tell how si - lent - ly He suf - fered, As with His
3. I can-not tell how He will win the na - tions, How He will
4. I can-not tell how all the lands shall wor - ship, When at His

love up - on the sons of men, Or, why, as Shep - herd,
peace He graced this place of tears, Or how His heart up -
claim His earth - ly he - ri - tage, How sa - tis - fy the
bid - ding e - v'ry storm is stilled, Or who can say how

He should seek the wan - der - ers, To bring them back, they know not how or
on the cross was bro - ken, The crown of pain to three and thir - ty
needs and a - spi - ra - tions Of East and West, of sin - ner and of
great the ju - bi - la - tion When all the hearts of men with love are

when: But this I know, that He was born of Ma - ry, When Beth-l'hem's
years: But this I know, He heals the bro - ken heart - ed, And stays our
sage: But this I know, all flesh shall see His glo - ry, And He shall
filled: But this I know, the skies will thrill with glad - ness, And my - riad,

man - ger was His on - ly home, And that He lived at Naz - a - reth and
sin and calms our lurk - ing fear, And lifts the bur - den from the hea - vy-
reap the har - vest He has sown, And some glad day His sun shall shine in
my - riad hu - man voic - es sing, And earth to heav'n, and heav'n to earth will

la - bored, And so the Sa - vior, Sa - vior of the world is come.
la - den, For yet the Sa - vior, Sa - vior of the world is here.
splen - dor When He the Sa - vior, Sa - vior of the world is known.
an - swer, At last the Sa - vior, Sa - vior of the world is King!

. . . for he is Lord of lords and King of kings/Rev 17:14

Benjamin R Hanby (1833-1867)

Marc Hedlin (1942-   )
Rich 7 7 7 7 w/refrain

1. Who   is   He   in   yon-der   stall,   At whose feet   the   shep-herds   fall?
2. Who   is   He   the   peo-ple   bless   For   His   words   of   gen-tle-ness?
3. Who   is   He   that stands and weeps   At   the   grave where Laz-arus sleeps?
4. Lo!   at   mid-night, who   is   He   Prays   in   dark Geth-se-ma-ne?
5. Who   is   He   who from the grave   Comes   to   heal   and   help   and   save?

(Major when Coda added)

Who   is   He   in   deep dis-tress,   Fast-ing   in   the   wil-der-ness?
Who   is   He   to whom they bring   All   the sick   and   sor-row-ing?
Who   is   He   the   ga-th'ring throng   Greet with loud tri-um-phant song?
Who   is   He   on   yon-der   tree   Dies   in grief and   a-go-ny?
Who   is   He   that from His throne   Rules through all   the world   a-lone?

Coda (after stanza 5 or 1, 3, 5)

'Tis   the   Lord!   O   won-drous sto-ry!   'Tis   the   Lord!   The   King   of   glo-ry!

At   His   feet   we   hum-bly   fall,   Crown Him! Crown Him, Lord of all!   A-men.

music: © 1976 Marc Hedlin, assigned to Inter-Varsity Christian Fellowship.

Empty He Came

His Life & Work

Jesus Christ, who . . . emptied himself/Phil 2:5, 7

Gavin Reid

Norman Warren (1934-   )
4 6 4 6 7 7

61 My Song Is Love Unknown

... the Son of God, who loved me and gave himself for me/Gal 2:20

Samuel Crossman (c1624-1683)

John Ireland (1879-1962)
Love Unknown 6 6 6 6 4 4 4 4

Unison

1. My song is love un - known, My Sa - vior's love to me, Love
2. He came from His blest throne, Sal - va - tion to be - stow; But
3. Some - times they strew His way, And His sweet prais - es sing; Re -
4. Why, what hath my Lord done? What makes this rage and spite? He
5. They rise, and needs will have My dear Lord made a - way; A
6. In life, no house, no home My Lord on earth might have; In
7. Here might I stay and sing, No sto - ry so di - vine; Ne -

to the love - less shown, That they might love - ly be. O
men made strange, and none The longed - for Christ would know. But
sound - ing all the day Ho - san - nas to their King. Then:
made the lame to run, He gave the blind their sight. Sweet
mur - der - er they save, The Prince of Life they slay. Yet
death no friend - ly tomb But what a stran - ger gave. What
ver was love, dear King, Ne - ver was grief like Thine. This

who am I, That for my sake My Lord should take frail flesh, and die?
O, my Friend, My Friend in - deed, Who at my need His life did spend!
'Cru - ci - fy!' Is all their breath, And for His death They thirst and cry.
in - ju - ries! Yet they at these Them - selves dis - please, And 'gainst Him rise.
cheer - ful He To suf - f'rings goes, That He His foes from thence might free.
may I say? Heav'n was His home; But mine the tomb Where - in He lay.
is my Friend, In whose sweet praise I all my days could glad - ly spend.

music: © by the Successor to the late Dr John Ireland. Used by permission.

62 Let Us Love, and Sing

His Life & Work

To him who loves us and has freed us . . . be glory and dominion/Rev 1:5-6

John Newton (1725-1807)

"Geistreiches Gesangbuch" Darmstadt (1698)
All Saints 8 7 8 7 7 7

1. Let us love, and sing, and won - der, Let us praise the
2. Let us love the Lord who bought us, Pi - tied us when
3. Let us sing, though fierce temp - ta - tions Threat - en hard to
4. Let us won - der; grace and jus - tice Join, and point to
5. Let us praise, and join the cho - rus Of the saints en -

Sa - vior's name! He has hushed the Law's loud thun - der,
e - ne - mies, Called us by His grace, and taught us,
bear us down! For the Lord, our strong sal - va - tion,
mer - cy's store; When through grace in Christ our trust is,
throned on high; Here they trust - ed Him be - fore us,

He has quenched Mount Si - nai's flame; He has washed us
Gave us ears, and gave us eyes: He has washed us
Holds in view the con - qu'ror's crown, He who washed us
Jus - tice smiles and asks no more: He who washed us
Now their prais - es fill the sky: 'Thou hast washed us

with His blood, He has brought us nigh to God.
with His blood, He pre - sents our souls to God.
with His blood, Soon will bring us home to God.
with His blood, Has se - cured our way to God.
with Thy blood; Thou art wor - thy, Lamb of God!' A - men.

63 O Sacred Head, Once Wounded

... and plaiting a crown of thorns they put it on his head/Mt 27:29

attr to Bernard of Clairvaux (c1150)
tr Paul Gerhardt (1607-1676)
tr James W Alexander (1804-1859)

Hans Leo Hassler (1564-1612)
arr J S Bach (1685-1750)
Passion Chorale 7 6 7 6 D

1. O sa-cred Head, once wound-ed, With grief and shame bow'd down,
2. What Thou, my Lord, hast suf-fered, Was all for sin-ners' gain;
3. What lan-guage shall I bor-row To thank Thee, dear-est Friend,
4. Be near me when I'm dy-ing, O show Thy cross to me;

Now scorn-ful-ly sur-round-ed With thorns, Thine on-ly crown.
Mine, mine was the trans-gres-sion, But Thine the dead-ly pain:
For this Thy dy-ing sor-row, Thy pi-ty with-out end?
And to my suc-cour fly-ing Come, Lord, and set me free.

O sa-cred Head, what glo-ry, What bliss till now was Thine!
Lo, here I fall, my Sa-vior! 'Tis I de-serve Thy place;
O make me Thine for e-ver; And should I faint-ing be,
These eyes new faith re-ceiv-ing, From Je-sus shall not move;

Yet, though des-pised and go-ry, I joy to call Thee mine.
Look on me with Thy fa-vor, Vouch-safe to me Thy grace.
Lord, let me ne-ver, ne-ver Out-live my love for Thee.
For he, who dies be-liev-ing, Dies safe-ly through Thy love. A-men.

64 O Christ, What Burdens

His Life & Work

... he loved us and sent his Son to be the expiation for our sins/1 Jn 4:10

Anne R Cousin (1824-1906)

Louis Spohr (1784-1859)
Spohr 8 6 8 6 8 6

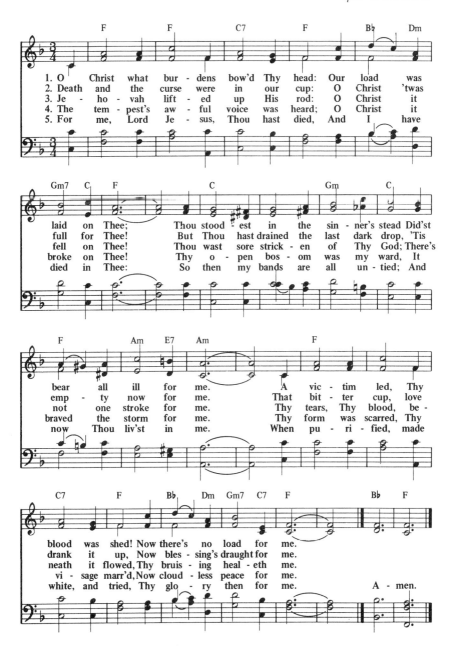

1. O Christ what bur - dens bow'd Thy head: Our load was
2. Death and the curse were in our cup: O Christ 'twas
3. Je - ho - vah lift - ed up His rod: O Christ it
4. The tem - pest's aw - ful voice was heard; O Christ it
5. For me, Lord Je - sus, Thou hast died, And I have

laid on Thee; Thou stood - est in the sin - ner's stead Did'st
full for Thee! But Thou hast drained the last dark drop, 'Tis
fell on Thee! Thou wast sore strick - en of Thy God; There's
broke on Thee! Thy o - pen bos - om was my ward, It
died in Thee: So then my bands are all un - tied; And

bear all ill for me. A vic - tim led, Thy
emp - ty now for me. That bit - ter cup, love
not one stroke for me. Thy tears, Thy blood, be -
braved the storm for me. Thy form was scarred, Thy
now Thou liv'st in me. When pu - ri - fied, made

blood was shed! Now there's no load for me.
drank it up, Now bles - sing's draught for me.
neath it flowed, Thy bruis - ing heal - eth me.
vi - sage marr'd, Now cloud - less peace for me.
white, and tried, Thy glo - ry then for me. A - men.

God the Son: *His kingdom, present and future*

Yea, Amen! let all adore Thee,
High on Thine eternal throne;
Savior, take the power and glory,
Claim the kingdom for Thine own;
Hallelujah! Hallelujah! Hallelujah!
O come quickly; come, Lord, come.

John Cennick
Charles Wesley
Martin Madan

65 Jesus Christ Is Risen

His Kingdom, Present & Future

The Lord has risen indeed/Lk 24:34

"Lyra Davidica" (1708)
"Supplement to the New Version" (c1816)

altered from melody in "Lyra Davidica" (1708)
Easter Hymn   7 7 7 7 w/Hallelujahs

1. Je - sus Christ is ris'n to - day, Hal - le - lu - jah!
2. Hymns of praise, then, let us sing Hal - le - lu - jah!
3. But the an - guish He en - dured Hal - le - lu - jah!

Our tri - um - phant ho - ly day, Hal - le - lu - jah!
Un - to Christ our heav'n - ly King, Hal - le - lu - jah!
Our sal - va - tion hath pro - cured; Hal - le - lu - jah!

Who did once up - on the cross, Hal - le - lu - jah!
Who en - dured the cross and grave, Hal - le - lu - jah!
Now a - bove the sky He's King, Hal - le - lu - jah!

Suf - fer to re - deem our loss. Hal - le - lu - jah!
Sin - ners to re - deem and save. Hal - le - lu - jah!
Where the an - gels e - ver sing. Hal - le - lu - jah! A - men.

66 Thou Art Coming

His Kingdom, Present & Future

Surely I am coming soon/Rev 22:20

Frances R Havergal (1836-1879)

William H Monk (1823-1889)
Beverley 8 7 8 8 7 7 7 7 7

1. Thou art com - ing, O my Sa - vior, Thou art com - ing,
2. Thou art com - ing, Thou art com - ing; We shall meet Thee
3. Thou art com - ing; at Thy Ta - ble We are wit - ness -
4. O the joy to see Thee reign - ing, Thee, my own be -

1. O my King, In Thy beau - ty all re - splen - dent, In Thy glo - ry
2. on Thy way, We shall see Thee, we shall know Thee, We shall bless Thee,
3. es for this; While re - mem - b'ring hearts Thou meet - est In com - mun - ion
4. lov - ed Lord! E - v'ry tongue Thy Name con - fes - sing, Wor - ship, hon - or,

1. all tran - scen - dent; Well may we re - joice and sing: Com - ing! in the
2. we shall show Thee All our hearts could ne - ver say: What an an - them
3. clear - est, sweet - est, Earn - est of our com - ing bliss, Show - ing not Thy
4. glo - ry, bles - sing Brought to Thee with glad ac - cord; Thee, my Mas - ter

1. open - ing east Her - ald bright - ness slow - ly swells; Com - ing!
2. that will be, Ring - ing out our love to Thee, Pour - ing
3. death a - lone, And Thy love ex - ceed - ing great, Vin - di - cat - ed and en - throned; Un - to
4. and my Friend, Vin - di - cat - ed and en - throned; Un - to

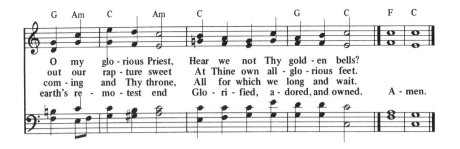

O my glo-rious Priest, Hear we not Thy gold-en bells?
out our rap-ture sweet At Thine own all-glo-rious feet.
com-ing and Thy throne, All for which we long and wait.
earth's re-mo-test end Glo-ri-fied, a-dored, and owned. A-men.

67 Christ Is Risen

His Kingdom, Present & Future

"The Lord has risen indeed"/Lk 24:30

Margaret Bowdler

Norman Warren (1934-   )
7 7 7 8

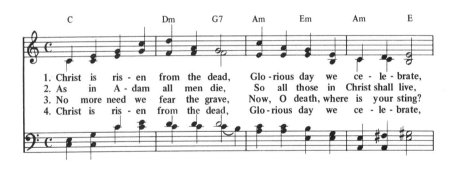

1. Christ is ris-en from the dead, Glo-rious day we ce-le-brate,
2. As in A-dam all men die, So all those in Christ shall live,
3. No more need we fear the grave, Now, O death, where is your sting?
4. Christ is ris-en from the dead, Glo-rious day we ce-le-brate,

Death has no pow'r o-ver Him, Hal-le-lu-jah, He is ris-en.
He has con-quer'd death and Hell, Hal-le-lu-jah, He is ris-en.
God gives us the vic-to-ry, Hal-le-lu-jah, He is ris-en.
Now we live thru faith in Him, Hal-le-lu-jah, He is ris-en.

68 When the Sun

His Kingdom, Present & Future

... the sun will be darkened, and the moon will not give its light/Mt 24:29

Christopher Idle (1938-   )

Norman Warren (1934-   )
Irregular

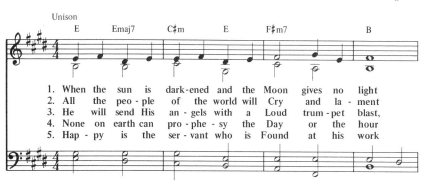

1. When the sun is dark-ened and the Moon gives no light
2. All the peo - ple of the world will Cry and la - ment
3. He will send His an - gels with a Loud trum - pet blast,
4. None on earth can pro - phe - sy the Day or the hour
5. Hap - py is the ser - vant who is Found at his work

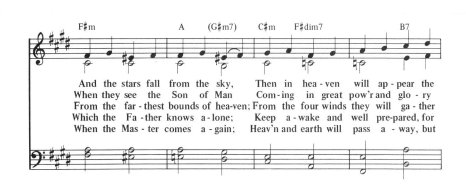

And the stars fall from the sky, Then in hea - ven will ap - pear the
When they see the Son of Man Com - ing in great pow'r and glo - ry
From the far - thest bounds of hea-ven; From the four winds they will ga - ther
Which the Fa - ther knows a - lone; Keep a - wake and well pre-pared, for
When the Mas - ter comes a - gain; Heav'n and earth will pass a - way, but

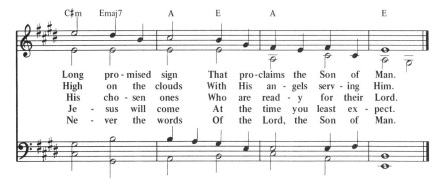

Long pro - mised sign That pro-claims the Son of Man.
High on the clouds With His an - gels serv - ing Him.
His cho - sen ones Who are read - y for their Lord.
Je - sus will come At the time you least ex - pect.
Ne - ver the words Of the Lord, the Son of Man.

69 Lo! He Comes

. . . every eye will see him/Rev 1:7

John Cennick (1718-1755)
Charles Wesley (1707-1788)
Martin Madan (1726-1790)

English Melody (18th century)
Helmsley 8 7 8 7 8 7

1. Lo! He comes, with clouds de-scend-ing, Once for fa-vored sin-ners slain; Thou-sand, thou-sand saints at-tend-ing Swell the tri-umph of His train; Hal-le-lu-jah! Hal-le-lu-jah! Hal-le-lu-jah! Christ ap-pears on earth to reign.

2. E-v'ry eye shall now be-hold Him, Robed in dread-ful ma-jes-ty; Those who set at naught and sold Him, Pierced, and nailed Him to the tree, Deep-ly wail-ing, Deep-ly wail-ing, Deep-ly wail-ing, Shall the true Mes-si-ah see.

3. Now re-demp-tion, long ex-pec-ted, See in so-lemn pomp ap-pear; All His saints, by man re-jec-ted, Now shall meet Him in the air. Hal-le-lu-jah! Hal-le-lu-jah! Hal-le-lu-jah! See the day of God ap-pear.

4. Yea, A-men! let all a-dore Thee, High on Thine e-ter-nal throne; Sa-vior, take the pow'r and glo-ry, Claim the king-dom for Thine own; Hal-le-lu-jah! Hal-le-lu-jah! Hal-le-lu-jah! O come quick-ly; come, Lord, come. A-men.

70 Then I Saw

His Kingdom, Present & Future

Then I saw a new heaven and a new earth/Rev 21:1

Christopher Idle (1938-   )

Norman Warren (1934-   )
Irregular

1. Then I saw a new heav'n and earth For the first had passed a-
2. He will wipe a-way e-v'ry tear, E-ven death shall die at
3. So the thir-sty can drink their fill At the foun-tain giv-ing
4. As they mea-sured its length and breadth I could see no tem-ple
5. And I saw by the sa-cred throne Flow-ing wa-ter, cry-stal

way, And the ho-ly ci-ty, came down from God, Like a
last; There'll be no more cry-ing, or grief, or pain, They be-
life; But the gates are shut on all e-vil things, On de-
there, For its on-ly tem-ple is God the Lord And the
clear, And the tree of life with its heal-ing leaves And its

bride on her wed-ding day. And I know how He loves His
long to a world that's past. And the One on the throne said
ceit and de-cay and strife. With foun-da-tions and walls and
Lamb in that ci-ty fair. And it needs nei-ther sun nor
fruit grow-ing all the year. So the wor-ship-pers of the

own For I heard His great voice tell, They would
'Look! I am ma-king all things new;' He is
tow'rs Like a jewel the ci-ty shines, With its
moon In a place which knows no night, For the
Lamb Bear His Name, and see His face; And they

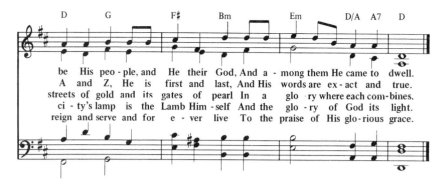

be His peo - ple, and He their God, And a - mong them He came to dwell.
A and Z, He is first and last, And His words are ex - act and true.
streets of gold and its gates of pearl In a glo - ry where each com-bines.
ci - ty's lamp is the Lamb Him - self And the glo - ry of God its light.
reign and serve and for e - ver live To the praise of His glo-rious grace.

71 Jesus Shall Reign   His Kingdom, Present & Future
... all nations serve him/Ps 72:11

Isaac Watts (1674-1748)   "Psalmodia Evangelica" (1789)
                                            Truro 8 8 8 8

1. Je - sus shall reign wher - e'er the sun Does his suc -
2. Bles - sings a - bound wher - e'er He reigns The pri - s'ner
3. To Him shall end - less prayer be made, And end - less
4. Peo - ple and realms of e - v'ry tongue Dwell on His

ces - sive jour - neys run; His king - dom spread from shore to
leaps to lose his chains; The wea - ry find e - ter - nal
prais - es crown His head; His name like sweet per - fume shall
love with sweet - est song, And in - fant voic - es shall pro -

shore, Till moons shall wax and wane no more.
rest, And all the sons of want are blest.
rise With e - v'ry morn - ing sac - ri - fice.
claim Their ear - ly bles - sings on His name. A - men.

72 At the Name of Jesus

His Kingdom, Present & Future

... at the name of Jesus every knee should bow/Phil 2:10

Caroline M Noel (1817-1877)

arr Marc Hedlin (1942-   )
Camberwell 6 5 6 5 D

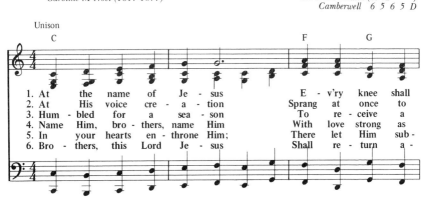

Unison

1. At the name of Je - sus
2. At His voice cre - a - tion
3. Hum - bled for a sea - son
4. Name Him, bro - thers, name Him
5. In your hearts en - throne Him;
6. Bro - thers, this Lord Je - sus

E - v'ry knee shall
Sprang at once to
To re - ceive a
With love strong as
There let Him sub -
Shall re - turn a -

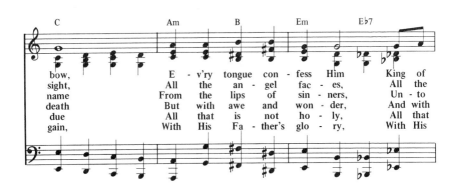

bow,
sight,
name
death
due
gain,

E - v'ry tongue con - fess Him
All the an - gel fac - es,
From the lips of sin - ners,
But with awe and won - der,
All that is not ho - ly,
With His Fa - ther's glo - ry,

King of
All the
Un - to
And with
All that
With His

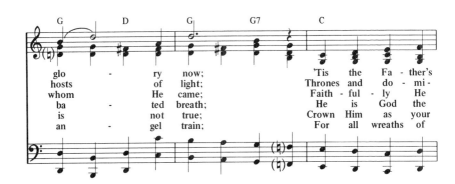

glo - ry now;
hosts of light;
whom He came;
ba - ted breath;
is not true;
an - gel train;

'Tis the Fa - ther's
Thrones and do - mi -
Faith - ful - ly He
He is God the
Crown Him as your
For all wreaths of

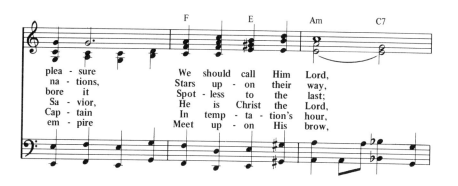

Chords: F E Am C7

plea - sure   We should call Him Lord,
na - tions,   Stars up - on their way,
bore it   Spot - less to the last;
Sa - vior,   He is Christ the Lord,
Cap - tain   In temp - ta - tion's hour,
em - pire   Meet up - on His brow,

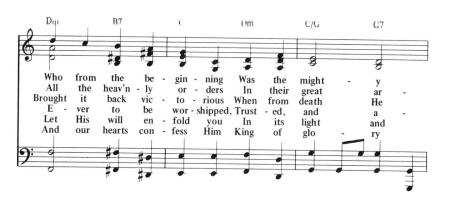

Chords: Dm B7 C Dm C/G G7

Who from the be - gin - ning   Was the might - y
All the heav'n - ly or - ders   In their great
Brought it back vic - to - rious   When from death
E - ver to be wor - shipped,   Trust - ed, and
Let His will en - fold you   In its light

And our hearts con - fess Him   King of glo - ry

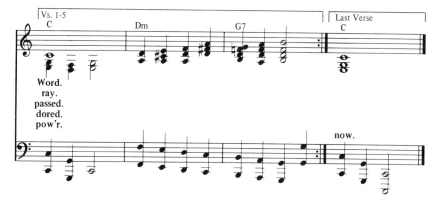

Vs. 1-5   Last Verse
C Dm G7   C

Word.
ray.
passed.
dored.
pow'r.   now.

73   Jerusalem the Golden   His Kingdom, Present & Future

... the holy city Jerusalem coming down out of heaven from God/Rev 21:10

Bernard of Cluny (c1145)
tr John M Neale (1818-1866) and others

Alexander Ewing (1830-1895)
Ewing   7 6 7 6 D

1. Je - ru - sa - lem the gold - en, With milk and hon - ey blest!
2. They stand, those halls of Zi - on, All ju - bi - lant with song,
3. There is the throne of Da - vid; And there, from care re - leased,
4. O sweet and bles - sed coun - try, The home of God's e - lect!

Be - neath thy con - tem - pla - tion Sink heart and voice op - pressed;
And bright with many an an - gel, And all the mar - tyr throng;
The song of them that tri - umph, The shout of them that feast;
O sweet and bles - sed coun - try That ea - ger hearts ex - pect!

I know not, O I know not What joys a - wait me there;
The Prince is e - ver in them, The day - light is se - rene;
And they, who with their Lead - er Have con - quered in the fight,
Je - sus, in mer - cy bring us To that dear land of rest;

What ra - dian - cy of glo - ry, What bliss be - yond com - pare!
The pas - tures of the bles - sed Are decked in glo - rious sheen.
For - e - ver and for - e - ver Are clad in robes of white.
Who art, with God the Fa - ther, And Spi - rit, e - ver blest. A - men.

74   Here from All Nations   His Kingdom, Present and Future

... behold, a great multitude which no man could number/Rev 7:9

Christopher Idle (1938-)

La Feillée, Methode (1808)
O Quanta Qualia   11 10 11 11

1. Here from all nations, all tongues, and all peoples
2. These have come out of the hardest oppression,
3. Gone is their thirst and no more shall they hunger,
4. He will go with them to clear living water
5. Blessing and glory and wisdom and power

Countless the crowd but their voices are one;
Now they may stand in the presence of God,
God is their shelter, His pow'r at their side;
Flowing from springs which His mercy supplies;
Be to the Saviour again and again;

Vast is the sight and majestic their singing —
Serving their Lord day and night in His temple,
Sun shall not pain them, no burning will torture,
Gone is their grief and their trials are over;
Might and thanksgiving and honour for ever

"God has the victory: He reigns from the throne."
Ransom'd and cleansed by the Lamb's precious blood.
Jesus the Lamb is their Shepherd and Guide.
God wipes away e'v'ry tear from their eyes.
Be to our God: Hallelujah! Amen.

God the Holy Spirit

For your gift of God the Spirit,
Power to make our lives anew,
Pledge of life and hope of glory,
Savior we would worship You.
Crowning gift of resurrection
Sent from Your ascended throne;
Fulness of the very Godhead
Come to make Your life our own.

E Margaret Clarkson

75   Gracious Spirit, Dwell with Me   God the Holy Spirit

... you know him, for he dwells with you, and will be in you/Jn 14:17

Thomas T Lynch (1818-1871)

Carole S Streeter (1934-)
Jonwold 7 7 7 7 7 7

1. Gra - cious Spi - rit, dwell with me! I my - self would gra - cious be; And with words that help and heal Would Thy life in mine re - veal; And with ac - tions bold and meek Would for Christ, my Sa - vior, speak.
2. Truth - ful Spi - rit, dwell with me! I my - self would truth - ful be; And with wis - dom kind and clear Let Thy life in mine ap - pear; And with ac - tions bro - ther - ly Speak my Lord's sin - ce - ri - ty.
3. Ten - der Spi - rit, dwell with me! I my - self would ten - der be; Shut my heart up like a flow'r In temp - ta - tion's dark - some hour; O - pen it when shines the sun, And His love by fra - grance own.
4. Ho - ly Spi - rit, dwell with me! I my - self would ho - ly be; Se - par - ate from sin I would Choose and cher - ish all things good, And what - e - ver I can be Give to Him who gave me Thee.

A - men.

music: © 1976 Carole S Streeter

... the Spirit of truth ... will guide you into all truth/Jn 16:13

E Margaret Clarkson (1915-   )   *Cyril Taylor (1907-   )*
                                                  Mead House 8 7 8 7 D

1. For your gift of God the Spi-rit, Pow'r to make our lives a-new,
2. He who in cre-a-tion's dawn-ing Brood-ed o'er the path-less deep,
3. He, Him-self the Liv-ing Au-thor, Wakes to life the sac-red Word,
4. He, the might-y God, in-dwells us; His to strength-en, help, em-pow-er,
5. Fa-ther, grant Your Ho-ly Spi-rit In our hearts may rule to-day,

Pledge of life and hope of glo-ry, Sa-vior we would wor-ship You.
Still a-cross our na-ture's dark-ness Moves to wake our souls from sleep;
Reads with us its ho-ly pa-ges And re-veals our ris-en Lord.
His to o-ver-come the Temp-ter—Ours to call in dan-ger's hour.
Grieved not, quenched not, but un-hin-dered Hold us in His might-y sway.

Crown-ing gift of re-sur-rec-tion, Sent from Your a-scend-ed throne;
Moves to stir, to draw, to quick-en, Thrusts us through with sense of sin;
He it is who works with-in us Teach-ing re-bel hearts to pray,
In His strength we dare to bat-tle All the ra-ging hosts of sin;
Fill us with Your ho-ly ful-ness, God the Fa-ther, Spi-rit, Son;

Ful-ness of the ve-ry God-head Come to make Your life our own.
Brings to birth and seals and fills us—Sav-ing Ad-vo-cate with-in.
He whose ho-ly in-ter-ces-sions Rise for us both night and day.
And by Him a-lone we con-quer Foes with-out and foes with-in.
In us, through us, then, for-e-ver, Shall Your per-fect will be done. A-men.

. . . that you may be filled with all the fulness of God/Eph 3:19

George Croly (1780-1860)

Frederick C Atkinson (1841-1897)
arr Hughes M Huffman (1942-   )
Morecambe   10 10 10 10

1. Spi - rit of God, de - scend up - on my heart;
2. I ask no dream, no pro - phet ec - sta - sies,
3. Hast Thou not bid us love Thee, God and King?
4. Teach me to feel that Thou art al - ways nigh;
5. Teach me to love Thee as Thine an - gels love,

Wean it from earth, through all its pul - ses move;
No sud - den rend - ing of the veil of clay,
All, all Thine own — soul, heart and strength and mind.
Teach me the strug - gles of the soul to bear,
One ho - ly pas - sion fil - ling all my frame;

Stoop to my weak - ness, might - y as Thou art,
No an - gel vi - sit - ant, no o - pening skies;
I see Thy cross — there teach my heart to cling.
To check the ris - ing doubt, the re - bel sigh;
The bap - tism of the heav'n de - scend - ed Dove;

And make me love Thee as I ought to love.
But take the dim - ness of my soul a - way.
Oh, let me seek Thee, and, oh, let me find.
Teach me the pa - tience of un - an - swered prayer.
My heart an al - tar, and Thy love the flame. A - men.

arrangement: © 1976 Hughes M Huffman, assigned to Inter-Varsity Christian Fellowship.

78 O for That Flame of Living Fire

God the Holy Spirit

... be filled with the Spirit/Eph 5:18

William Bathhurst (1796-1877)
adpt Mark Hunt (1951-)

William Smallwood (1831-1897)
Antwerp 8 8 8 8

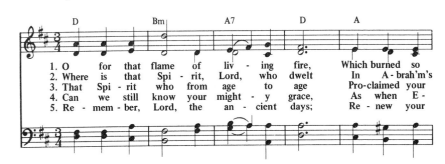

1. O for that flame of liv - ing fire, Which burned so
2. Where is that Spi - rit, Lord, who dwelt In A - brah'm's
3. That Spi - rit who from age to age Pro - claimed your
4. Can we still know your might - y grace, As when E -
5. Re - mem - ber, Lord, the an - cient days; Re - new your

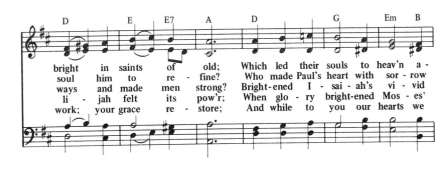

bright in saints of old; Which led their souls to heav'n a -
soul him to re - fine? Who made Paul's heart with sor - row
ways and made men strong? Bright-ened I - sai - ah's vi - vid
li - jah felt its pow'r; When glo - ry bright-ened Mos - es'
work; your grace re - store; And while to you our hearts we

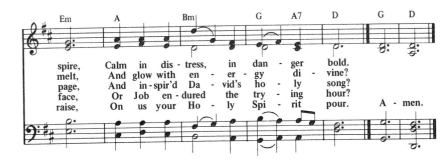

spire, Calm in dis - tress, in dan - ger bold.
melt, And glow with en - er - gy di - vine?
page, And in-spir'd Da - vid's ho - ly song?
face, Or Job en - dured the try - ing hour?
raise, On us your Ho - ly Spi - rit pour. A - men.

The Spirit Came, As Promised

God the Holy Spirit

In him you ... were sealed with the promised Holy Spirit/Eph 1:13

Jim Seddon

Norman Warren (1934-   )
7 6 7 6 D

1. The Spi - rit came, as pro - mised, In God's ap - point - ed hour; And
2. The Spi - rit makes our bo - dies The tem - ple of the Lord, He
3. He bids us live to - geth - er In un - i - ty and peace; Em -
4. The Word, the Spi - rit's wea - pon, Will bring all sin to light; And

now to each be - liev - er He comes in love and pow'r. And
binds us all to - geth - er In faith and true ac - cord. The
ploy His gifts in bles - sing, And let base pas - sions cease. We
prayer by His di - rect - ing, Will add new joy and might. Be

by His Ho - ly Spi - rit, God seals us as His own; And
Spi - rit in His great - ness, Brings pow'r from God a - bove, And
should not grieve the Spi - rit By o - pen sin or shame; Nor
filled then with His Spi - rit, Live out God's Will and Word; Re -

through the Son and Spi - rit Makes ac - cess to His throne.
with the Son and Fa - ther Dwells in our hearts in love.
let our words and ac - tions De - ny His Ho - ly Name.
joice with hymns and sing - ing, Make mu - sic to the Lord. A - men.

80 **Thrice Blessed Spirit** God the Holy Spirit

But the fruit of the Spirit is love, joy, peace/Gal 5:22

James Mountain (1843-1933) *James Mountain (1843-1933)*
  10 10 11 10

1. Thrice bles-sed Spi-rit! Giv-er of sal-va-tion
2. Thy sev-en-fold grace be-stow up-on us free-ly,
3. Make us long suf-f'ring. 'mid earth's pro-vo-ca-tion,
4. Meek-ness be-stow, with hum-ble self a-base-ment,
5. Then with the gift of ho-li-ness with-in us;

Pur-chased by Je-sus on the cross of shame;
Love, deep and full to God and all man-kind;
Gen-tle-ness give us, when en-dur-ing wrong;
And self-con-trol, through Thy con-trol-ling might;
We not less hu-man, but made more di-vine;

Fill all our hearts, trans-form them with Thy beau-ty—
Joy in the Lord, 'mid e-v'ry earth-ly sor-row;
Good-ness im-part, that we e'en foes may suc-cour;
And as we yield to e-v'ry call of du-ty,
Our lives re-plete with heav'ns su-per-nal beau-ty,

Fair-est a-dorn-ing of our Sa-vior's Name.
Peace, calm and sweet, that guard-eth heart and mind.
Faith-ful-ness grant, to change our toil to song.
May we do all as in Thy search-ing sight.
E-ver de-clare, that beau-ty, Lord is Thine. A-men.

81   O Spirit of the Living God

But when the counselor comes . . . he will bear witness to me/Jn 15:26

James Montgomery (1771-1854)

Samuel Webbe (1740-1816)
Melcombe   8 8 8 8

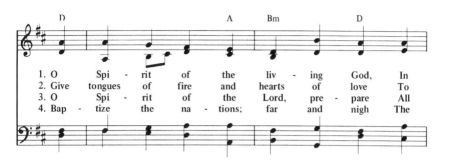

1. O Spi - rit of the liv - ing God, In
2. Give tongues of fire and hearts of love To
3. O Spi - rit of the Lord, pre - pare All
4. Bap - tize the na - tions; far and nigh The

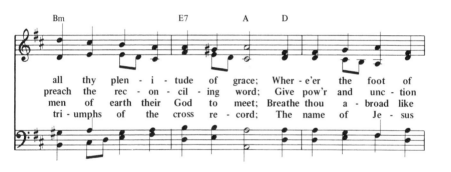

all thy plen - i - tude of grace; Wher - e'er the foot of
preach the rec - on - cil - ing word; Give pow'r and unc - tion
men of earth their God to meet; Breathe thou a - broad like
tri - umphs of the cross re - cord; The name of Je - sus

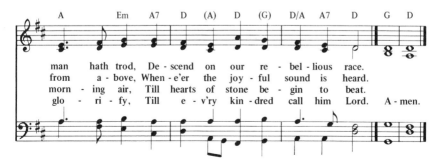

man hath trod, De - scend on our re - bel - lious race.
from a - bove, When - e'er the joy - ful sound is heard.
morn - ing air, Till hearts of stone be - gin to beat.
glo - ri - fy, Till e - v'ry kin - dred call him Lord. A - men.

82 Holy Spirit, Truth Divine

... strengthened with might through his Spirit in the inner man/Eph 3:16

Samuel Longfellow (1819-1892)

Freylinghausen's "Gesangbuch" (1704)
Lübeck 7 7 7 7

1. Ho - ly Spi - rit, truth Di - vine, Dawn up - on this soul of mine;
2. Ho - ly Spi - rit, love Di - vine, Glow with - in this heart of mine;
3. Ho - ly Spi - rit, pow'r Di - vine, Fill and nerve this will of mine;
4. Ho - ly Spi - rit, right Di - vine, King with - in my con-science reign;
5. Ho - ly Spi - rit, peace Di - vine, Still this rest - less heart of mine,
6. Ho - ly Spi - rit, joy Di - vine, Glad - den Thou this heart of mine;

Word of God, and in - ward light, Wake my spi - rit, clear my sight.
Kin - dle e - v'ry high de - sire, Per - ish self in Thy pure fire.
By Thee may I strong-ly live, Brave - ly bear, and no - bly strive.
Be my Lord, and I shall be Firm - ly bound, for e - ver free.
Speak to calm this tos - sing sea, Stayed in Thy tran-quil - li - ty.
In the de - sert ways I'll sing: Spring, O Well, for e - ver spring! A - men.

83 Come, Holy Ghost

God's love has been poured into our hearts through the Holy Spirit/Rom 5:5

Charles Wesley (1707-1788)

Este's "The Whole Book of Psalms" (1592)
Winchester Old 8 6 8 6

1. Come, Ho - ly Ghost, our hearts in - spire, Let us thine in-fluence prove: Source
2. Come, Ho - ly Ghost, for moved by thee The pro - phets wrote and spoke; Un -
3. Ex - pand thy wings, ce - les - tial Dove, Brood o'er our na - ture's night; On
4. God, thru him - self, we then shall know If thou with - in us shine, And

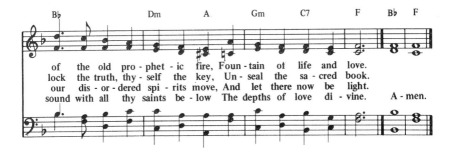

of the old pro - phet - ic fire, Foun - tain of life and love.
lock the truth, thy - self the key, Un - seal the sa - cred book.
our dis - or - dered spi - rits move, And let there now be light.
sound with all thy saints be - low The depths of love di - vine. A - men.

84 Our Blest Redeemer

God the Holy Spirit

And I will pray the Father, and he will give you another Counselor/Jn 14:16

Harriet Auber (1773-1862)

John B Dykes (1823-1876)
St Cuthbert 8 6 8 4

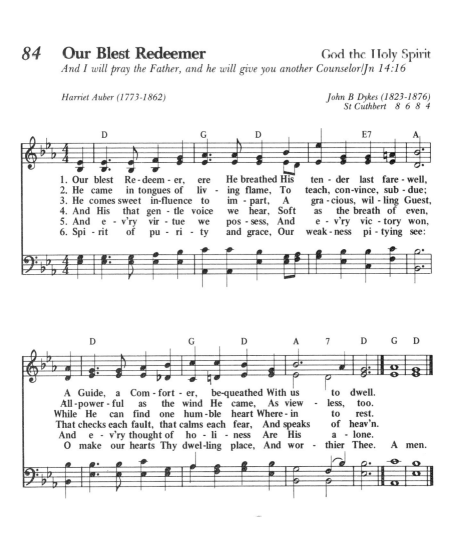

1. Our blest Re - deem - er, ere He breathed His ten - der last fare - well,
2. He came in tongues of liv - ing flame, To teach, con - vince, sub - due;
3. He comes sweet in - fluence to im - part, A gra - cious, wil - ling Guest,
4. And His that gen - tle voice we hear, Soft as the breath of even,
5. And e - v'ry vir - tue we pos - sess, And e - v'ry vic - tory won,
6. Spi - rit of pu - ri - ty and grace, Our weak - ness pi - tying see:

A Guide, a Com - fort - er, be - queathed With us to dwell.
All - power - ful as the wind He came, As view - less, too.
While He can find one hum - ble heart Where - in to rest.
That checks each fault, that calms each fear, And speaks of heav'n.
And e - v'ry thought of ho - li - ness Are His a - lone.
O make our hearts Thy dwel - ling place, And wor - thier Thee. A men.

Life in Christ

Jesus Christ is Lord today.
Walk, then, in His Way!
Guardian and instructor, He
Makes our sin-closed eyes to see;
He maintains our human needs
And our inner longing heeds;
Jesus Christ is Lord today.
Walk, then, in His Way!

W Keith Weathers

85 Jesus, Lover of My Soul

Repentance & Forgiveness

For thou hast been . . . a shelter from the storm/Is 25:4

Charles Wesley (1708-1788)

Joseph Parry (1841-1903)
Aberystwyth 7 7 7 7 D

1. Je - sus, Lov - er of my soul, Let me to Thy bos - om fly,
2. Oth - er ref - uge have I none; Hangs my help - less soul on Thee;
3. Thou, O Christ, art all I want; More than all in Thee I find;
4. Plen - teous grace with Thee is found, Grace to cov - er all my sin;

While the near - er wa - ters roll, While the tem - pest still is high:
Leave, ah! leave me not a - lone, Still sup - port and com - fort me.
Raise the fal - len, cheer the faint, Heal the sick, and lead the blind.
Let the heal - ing streams a - bound; Make and keep me pure with - in.

Hide me, O my Sa - vior, hide, Till the storm of life is past;
All my trust on Thee is stayed, All my help from Thee I bring;
Just and ho - ly is Thy name, I am all un - right - eous - ness;
Thou of life the foun - tain art, Free - ly let me take of Thee;

Safe in - to the ha - ven guide; O re - ceive my soul at last!
Cov - er my de - fense - less head With the sha - dow of Thy wing.
False and full of sin I am, Thou art full of truth and grace.
Spring Thou up with - in my heart, Rise to all e - ter - ni - ty. A - men.

86 Out of the Depths

Repentance & Forgiveness

Out of the depths I cry to thee, O LORD!/Ps 130:1

Martin Luther (1483-1546)
tr Benjamin Latrobe (1725-1786)

Walther's "Geistliches Gesangbüchlein" Wittenberg (1524)
arr J S Bach (1685-1750)
Aus Tieffer Not 8 7 8 7 8 8 7

1. Out of the depths I cry to thee: Lord, hear me, I im-plore thee; Bend down thy gra-cious ear to me, Let my prayer come be-fore thee! On my mis-deeds in mer-cy look, O deign to blot them from thy book.

2. Thy sov-'reign grace and bound-less love Show thee, O Lord for-giv-ing; My pur-est thoughts and deeds but prove Sin in my heart is liv-ing: None guilt-less in thy sight ap-pear, All who ap-proach thy throne must fear.

3. Thou canst be mer-ci-ful while just, This is my hope's foun-da-tion; In thy re-deem-ing grace I trust, O grant me thy sal-va-tion. Up-held by thee I stand se-cure: Thy word is firm, thy pro-mise sure,

4. Like those who watch for mid-night's hour To hail the dawn-ing mor-row, I wait for thee, I trust thy pow'r, Un-moved by doubt or sor-row. So let thy peo-ple hope in thee, And they shall find thy mer-cy free,

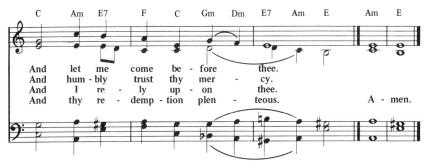

And let me come be - fore thee.
And hum - bly trust thy mer - cy.
And I re - ly up - on thee.
And thy re - demp - tion plen - teous. A - men.

87 Jesus, Thy Blood

Repentance & Forgiveness

... he has clothed me with the garments of salvation/Is 61:10

Nicolaus L von Zinzendorf (1700-1760)
tr John Wesley (1703-1791)

Gardiner's "Sacred Melodies" (1815)
Germany 8 8 8 8

1. Je - sus, Thy blood and right - eous - ness My beau - ty are, my
2. Bold shall I stand in Thy great day, For who aught to my
3. Lord, I be - lieve Thy pre - cious blood, Which, at the mer - cy -
4. Lord, I be - lieve were sin - ners more Than sands up - on the

glo - rious dress; 'Midst flam - ing worlds, in these ar -
charge shall lay? Ful - ly ab - solved through those I
seat of God, For - e - ver doth for sin - ners
o - cean shore, Thou hast for all a ran - som

rayed, With joy shall I lift up my head.
am, From sin and fear, from guilt and shame.
plead, For me, e'en for my soul, was shed.
paid, For all a full a - tone - ment made. A - men.

88 And Can It Be

Repentance & Forgiveness

... while we were yet sinners Christ died for us/Rom 5:8

Charles Wesley (1707-1788)

Thomas Campbell (1777-1844)
Sagina 8 8 8 8 D

1. And can it be that I should gain An in-t'rest in the
2. 'Tis mys-t'ry all! Th'Im-mor-tal dies: Who can ex-plore His
3. He left His Fa-ther's throne a-bove, So free, so in-fi-
4. Long my im-pri-son'd spi-rit lay Fast bound in sin and
5. No con-dem-na-tion now I dread; Je-sus, and all in

Sa-vior's blood? Died He for me, who caused His pain? For me, who
strange de-sign? In vain the first-born ser-aph tries To sound the
nite His grace, Emp-tied Him-self of all but love, And bled for
na-ture's night; Thine eye dif-fused a quick-'ning ray, I woke, the
Him, is mine! A-live in Him, my liv-ing Head, And clothed in

Him to death pur-sued? A-maz-ing love! how can it be That
depths of love di-vine. 'Tis mer-cy all! let earth a-dore, Let
A-dam's help-less race. 'Tis mer-cy all, im-mense and free; For,
dun-geon flamed with light; My chains fell off, my heart was free, I
right-eous-ness di-vine, Bold I ap-proach th'e-ter-nal throne, And

Thou, my God, shouldst die for me? A-maz-ing love! how
an-gel minds in-quire no more. 'Tis mer-cy all! let
O my God, it found out me! 'Tis mer-cy all, im-
rose, went forth, and fol-lowed Thee. My chains fell off, my
claim the crown, through Christ, my own. Bold I ap-proach th'e-

A-maz-ing love!

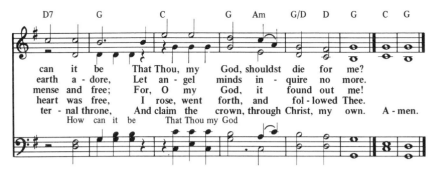

can it be That Thou, my God, shouldst die for me?
earth a - dore, Let an - gel minds in - quire no more.
mense and free; For, O my God, it found out me!
heart was free, I rose, went forth, and fol - lowed Thee.
ter - nal throne, And claim the crown, through Christ, my own. A - men.

How can it be That Thou my God

89 I Sought the Lord

Repentance & Forgiveness

... those who are called ... and kept for Jesus Christ/Jude 1

The Pilgrim Hymnal (1904)   George W. Chadwick (1854-1931)
10 10 10 6

1. I sought the Lord, and af - ter - ward I knew He moved my
2. Thou didst reach forth Thy hand and mine en - fold; I walked and
3. I find, I walk, I love; but O the whole Of love is

soul to seek Him, seek - ing me; It was not I that
sank not on the storm-vexed sea; 'Twas not so much that
but my an - swer, Lord, to Thee! For Thou were long be -

found, O Sa - vior true; No, I was found of Thee.
I on Thee took hold, As Thou, dear Lord, on me.
fore-hand with my soul; Al - ways Thou lov - edst me. A - men.

90 Kind and Merciful God

Repentance & Forgiveness

If we confess our sins, he is faithful and just, and will forgive/1 Jn 1:9

Bryan J Leech (1931-   )

Swedish melody
Elfåker 6 6 9 D

1. Kind and mer-ci-ful God, we have sinned in your sight,
2. Kind and mer-ci-ful God, we've ne-glect-ed your Word
3. Kind and mer-ci-ful God, we have bro-ken your laws
4. Kind and mer-ci-ful God, in Christ's death on the cross
5. Kind and mer-ci-ful God, bid us lift up our heads

We have all wan-dered far from your way;
And the truth that would guide us a-right;
And in con-duct have veered from the norm;
You pro-vid-ed a cleans-ing from sin;
And com-mand us to rise from our knees;

We have fol-lowed de-sire, We have failed to a-spire
We have lived in the shade Of the dark we have made,
We have dreamed of the good, But the good that we could
Speak the words that for-give That hence-forth we may live
May our hearts now be changed And no long-er es-tranged,

To the vir-tue we ought to dis-play.
When you willed us to walk in the light.
We have fre-quent-ly failed to per-form.
By the might of your Spi-rit with-in.
Through the pow'r of your par-don and peace. A-men.

91 Lord, I Was Blind

Repentance & Forgiveness

And you he made alive, when you were dead/Eph 2:1

William T Matson (1833-1899)

Alfred Scott-Gatty (1847-1918)
Bodmin 8 8 8 8

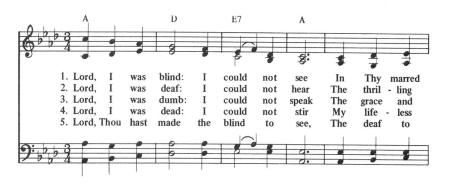

1. Lord, I was blind: I could not see In Thy marred
2. Lord, I was deaf: I could not hear The thril - ling
3. Lord, I was dumb: I could not speak The grace and
4. Lord, I was dead: I could not stir My life - less
5. Lord, Thou hast made the blind to see, The deaf to

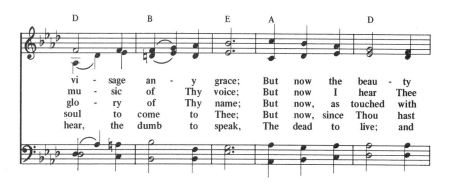

vi - sage an - y grace; But now the beau - ty
mu - sic of Thy voice; But now I hear Thee
glo - ry of Thy name; But now, as touched with
soul to come to Thee; But now, since Thou hast
hear, the dumb to speak, The dead to live; and

of Thy face   In ra-diant vi - sion dawns on me.
and re - joice,   And all Thine ut - tered words are dear.
liv - ing flame, My lips Thine ea - ger prais - es wake.
quick - ened me, I rise from sin's dark sep - ul - chre.
lo, I break   The chains of my cap - ti - vi - ty! A - men.

music: by permission of the Abbot of Downside.

92   We Have Not Known Thee   Repentance & Forgiveness

I have gone astray like a lost sheep; seek thy servant/Ps 119:176

Thomas B Pollock (1836-1896)

Sir Joseph Barnby (1838-1896)
arr Marc Hedlin (1942-   )
St Chrysostom   8 8 8 8 8 8

1. We have not known Thee as we ought, Nor learned Thy wis - dom,
2. We have not feared Thee as we ought, Nor bowed be - neath Thine
3. We have not loved Thee as we ought, Nor cared that we are
4. We have not served Thee as we ought; A - las, the du - ties
5. When shall we know Thee as we ought, And fear, and love, and

grace, and pow'r; The things of earth have filled our thought, And
awe - ful eye, Nor guard - ed deed, and word, and thought, Re -
loved by Thee; Thy pres - ence we have cold - ly sought, And
left un - done, The work with lit - tle fer - vor wrought, The
serve a - right? When shall we, out of tri - al brought, Be

tri - fles of the pas - sing hour. Lord, give us light Thy
mem - b'ring that our God was nigh. Lord, give us faith to
feeb - ly longed Thy face to see. Lord, give a pure and
bat - tles lost or scarce - ly won! Lord, give the zeal, and
per - fect in the land of light? Lord, may we day by

truth to see, And make us wise in know - ing Thee.
know Thee near, And grant the grace of ho - ly fear.
lov - ing heart To feel and own the love Thou art.
give the might, For Thee to toil, for Thee to fight.
day pre - pare To see Thy face, and serve Thee there. A - men.

arrangement: © 1976 Marc Hedlin, assigned to Inter-Varsity Christian Fellowship.

In him we have redemption through his blood/Eph 1:7

John S B Monsell (1811-1875)

Anon
7 6 7 6 D

1. My sins, my sins, my Sa - vior! They take such hold on me,
I am not a - ble to look up, Save on - ly Christ to Thee;
In Thee is all for - give - ness, In Thee a - bun - dant grace,
My sha - dow and my sun - shine The bright - ness of Thy face.

2. My sins, my sins, my Sa - vior! How sad on Thee they fall;
Seen through Thy gen - tle pa - tience, I ten - fold feel them all;
I know they are for - giv - en, But still, their pain to me
Is all the grief and an - guish They laid, my Lord, on Thee.

3. My sins, my sins, my Sa - vior! Their guilt I ne - ver knew
Till with Thee in the des - ert I near Thy pas - sion drew;
Till with Thee in the gar - den I heard Thy plead - ing prayer,
And saw the sweat - drops blood - y That told Thy sor - row there.

4. There - fore my songs, my Sa - vior, E'en in this time of woe,
Shall tell of all Thy good - ness To suf - f'ring man be - low;
Thy good - ness and Thy fa - vor, Whose pres - ence from a - bove
Re - joice those hearts my Sa - vior, That live in Thee a - lone. A - men.

94 Just As I Am

. . . him who comes to me I will not cast out/Jn 6:37

Charlotte Elliott (1789-1871)

Henry Smart (1813-1879)
Misericordia 8 8 8 6

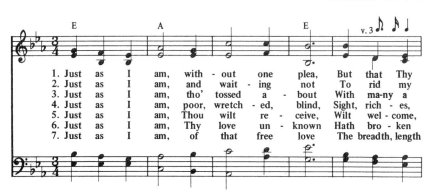

1. Just as I   am,   with - out   one   plea,   But   that   Thy
2. Just as I   am,   and   wait - ing   not   To   rid   my
3. Just as I   am,   tho' tossed   a - bout   With   ma-ny a
4. Just as I   am,   poor, wretch - ed,   blind,   Sight, rich - es,
5. Just as I   am,   Thou   wilt   re - ceive,   Wilt   wel - come,
6. Just as I   am,   Thy   love   un - known   Hath   bro - ken
7. Just as I   am,   of   that   free   love   The breadth, length

blood was shed for me,   And that Thou bid'st me
soul of one dark blot,   To Thee, whose blood can
con - flict, ma-ny a doubt,   Fight - ings with - in, and
heal - ing of the mind,   Yea, all I need, in
par - don, cleanse, re - lieve;   Be - cause Thy pro - mise
e - v'ry bar - rier down;   Now to be Thine, yea
depth, the height to prove,   Here for a sea - son

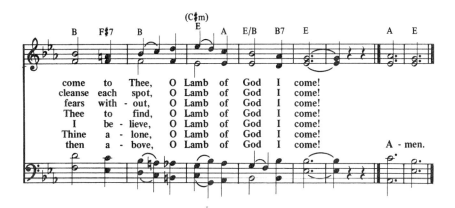

come to Thee, O Lamb of God I come!
cleanse each spot, O Lamb of God I come!
fears with - out, O Lamb of God I come!
Thee to find, O Lamb of God I come!
I   be - lieve, O Lamb of God I come!
Thine a - lone, O Lamb of God I come!
then a - bove, O Lamb of God I come!

A - men.

Souls of Men   Repentance & Forgiveness

I am the good shepherd/Jn 10:11

Frederick W Faber (1814-1863)

Arthur H Brown (1830-1926)
St Mabyn   8 7 8 7

1. Souls of men, why will ye scat - ter Like a crowd of
2. Was there e - ver kind - est shep - herd Half so gen - tle,
3. There's a wide - ness in God's mer - cy Like the wide - ness
4. There is wel - come for the sin - ner, And more grac - es
5. There is plen - ti - ful re - demp - tion In the blood that
6. For the love of God is broad - er Than the mea - sures
7. But we make His love too nar - row By false li - mits
8. If our love were but more sim - ple We should take Him

fright - ened sheep? Fool - ish hearts, why will ye wan - der
half so sweet, As the Sa - vior who would have us
of the sea, There's a kind - ness in His jus - tice
for the good; There is mer - cy with the Sav - ior
has been shed; There is joy for all the mem - bers
of man's mind; And the heart of the E - ter - nal
of our own; And we mag - ni - fy its strict - ness
at His word: And our lives would be all sun - shine

From a love so true and deep?
Come and ga - ther round His feet?
Which is more than li - ber - ty.
There is heal - ing in His blood.
In the sor - row of the Head.
Is most won - der - ful - ly kind.
With a zeal He will not own.
In the sweet - ness of our Lord.   A - men.

by permission of Oxford University Press.

96 My Faith Has Found a Resting Place

... while we were yet sinners Christ died for us/Rom 5:8

Lidie H Edmunds (19th century)

Norse Melody
arr William J Kirkpatrick (1838-1921)
Landas 8 6 8 6 w/refrain

1. My faith has found a rest-ing-place, Not in de-vice nor creed;
2. E-nough for me that Je-sus saves, This ends my fear and doubt;
3. My heart is lean-ing on the Word, The writ-ten Word of God,
4. My great Phy-si-cian heals the sick, The lost He came to save;

I trust the E-ver-liv-ing One, His wounds for me shall plead.
A sin-ful soul I come to Him, He'll ne-ver cast me out.
Sal-va-tion by my Sa-vior's name, Sal-va-tion thro' His blood.
For me His pre-cious blood He shed, For me His life He gave.

I need no oth-er ar-gu-ment, I need no oth-er plea,

It is e-nough that Je-sus died, And that He died for me. A-men.

Jesus Lives, and So Shall I   Faith

. . . I am alive for evermore/Rev 1:18

Christian F Gellert (1715-1769)
tr Philip Schaff (c1870)

Johann Crüger (1598-1662)
Zuversicht 7 8 7 8 7 7

1. Je - sus lives and so shall I. Death! thy sting is
2. Je - sus lives and reigns su - preme; And, His king - dom
3. Je - sus lives, I know full well, Naught from Him my
4. Je - sus lives, and by His grace, Vic - t'ry o'er my
5. Je - sus lives, and death is now But my en - trance

gone for - e - ver, He who deigned for me to die,
still re - main - ing, I shall al - so be with Him,
heart can se - ver, Life nor death nor pow'rs of hell,
pas - sions giv - ing, I will cleanse my heart and ways,
in - to glo - ry. Cou - rage then, my soul, for thou

Lives the bands of death to se - ver. He shall raise me
E - ver liv - ing, e - ver reign - ing. God has pro - mised:
Joy nor grief hence - forth for - e - ver. None of all His
E - ver to His glo - ry liv - ing. Me He rais - es
Hast a crown of life be - fore thee; Thou shall find thy

with the just; Je - sus is my Hope and Trust.
be it must; Je - sus is my Hope and Trust.
saints is lost; Je - sus is my Hope and Trust.
from the dust; Je - sus is my Hope and Trust.
hopes were just; Je - sus is the Chris - tian's Trust. A - men.

98   Like a River Glorious   Faith

Then your peace would have been like a river/Is 48:18

Frances R Havergal (1836-1879)

James Mountain (1844-1933)
Wye Valley   6 5 6 5 D w/refrain

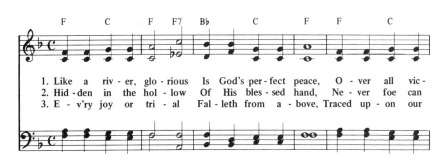

1. Like a riv-er, glo-rious Is God's per-fect peace, O-ver all vic-
2. Hid-den in the hol-low Of His bles-sed hand, Ne-ver foe can
3. E-v'ry joy or tri-al Fal-leth from a-bove, Traced up-on our

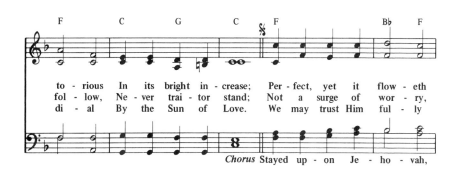

to-rious In its bright in-crease; Per-fect, yet it flow-eth
fol-low, Ne-ver trai-tor stand; Not a surge of wor-ry,
di-al By the Sun of Love. We may trust Him ful-ly

Chorus Stayed up-on Je-ho-vah,

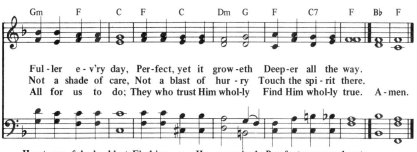

Ful-ler e-v'ry day, Per-fect, yet it grow-eth Deep-er all the way.
Not a shade of care, Not a blast of hur-ry Touch the spi-rit there.
All for us to do; They who trust Him whol-ly Find Him whol-ly true. A-men.

Hearts are ful-ly blest; Find-ing, as He pro-mised, Per-fect peace and rest.

99 Jesus, I Am Resting, Resting

Faith

... looking to Jesus the pioneer and perfecter of our faith/Heb 12:2

Jean S Pigott (1845-1882)

James Mountain (1844-1933)
Tranquillity 8 7 8 5 D w/refrain

1. Je - sus, I am rest - ing, rest - ing In the joy of what Thou art;
2. O, how great Thy lov - ing kind - ness, Vast - er, broad - er than the sea!
3. Sim - ply trust - ing Thee, Lord Je - sus, I be - hold Thee as Thou art,
4. E - ver lift Thy face up - on me As I work and wait for Thee;
(ref.) Je - sus, I am rest - ing, rest - ing In the joy of what Thou art;

I am find - ing out the great - ness Of Thy lov - ing heart.
O, how mar - vel - ous Thy good - ness, La - vished all on me!
And Thy love, so pure, so change - less, Sa - tis - fies my heart;
Rest - ing 'neath Thy smile, Lord Je - sus, Earth's dark sha - dows flee.
I am find - ing out the great - ness Of Thy lov - ing heart.

Thou hast bid me gaze up - on Thee, And Thy beau - ty fills my soul,
Yes, I rest in Thee, Be - lov - ed, Know what wealth of grace is Thine,
Sa - tis - fies its deep - est long - ings, Meets, sup - plies its e - v'ry need,
Bright - ness of my Fa - ther's glo - ry, Sun - shine of my Fa - ther's face,

For by Thy trans - form - ing pow - er, Thou hast made me whole.
Know Thy cer - tain - ty of pro - mise, And have made it mine.
Com - pas - seth me round with bles - sings: Thine is love in - deed!
Keep me e - ver trust - ing, rest - ing, Fill me with Thy grace.

100 Praise the Savior, Ye Who Know Him

Faith

Jesus Christ is the same yesterday and today and for ever/Heb 13:8

Thomas Kelly (1769-1855)

Traditional German Melody
Acclaim 8 8 8 5

1. Praise the Sav-ior, ye who know Him! Who can tell how much we owe Him?
2. Je - sus is the name that charms us; He for con-flict fits and arms us;
3. Trust in Him, ye saints, for - e - ver; He is faith-ful, chang-ing ne - ver;
4. Keep us, Lord, O keep us cleav-ing To Thy-self and still be - liev - ing;
5. Then we shall be where we would be, Then we shall be what we should be;

Glad - ly let us ren - der to Him All we are and have.
No-thing moves and no-thing harms us While we trust in Him.
Nei-ther force nor guile can se - ver Those He loves from Him.
Till the hour of our re - ceiv - ing Pro-mised joys with Thee.
Things that are not now, nor could be, Soon shall be our own. A - men.

101 I Am Not Skilled to Understand

Faith

God exalted him at his right hand as . . . Savior/Acts 5:31

Dora Greenwell (1821-1882)

William Kirkpatrick (1838-1921)
Greenwell 8 8 8 7

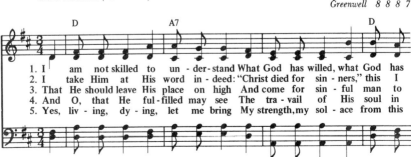

1. I am not skilled to un - der-stand What God has willed, what God has
2. I take Him at His word in - deed: "Christ died for sin - ners," this I
3. That He should leave His place on high And come for sin - ful man to
4. And O, that He ful - filled may see The tra - vail of His soul in
5. Yes, liv - ing, dy - ing, let me bring My strength, my sol - ace from this

planned; I on-ly know at His right hand Is One who is my Sa-vior!
read; For in my heart I find a need Of Him to be my Sa-vior!
die, You count it strange? so once did I, Be - fore I knew my Sa-vior!
me, And with His work con-tent-ed be, As I with my dear Sa-vior!
spring; That He who lives to be my King Once died to be my Sa-vior! A-men.

102 I Hear the Words of Love

Faith

... since we are justified by faith, we have peace with God/Rom 5:1

Horatius Bonar (1808-1889)

"Genevan Psalter" (1551)
St Michael   6 6 8 6

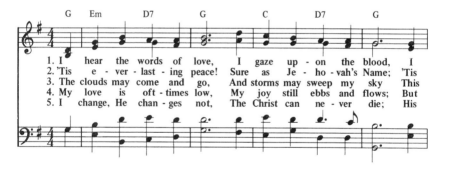

1. I   hear   the   words   of   love,   I   gaze   up - on   the   blood,   I
2. 'Tis   e - ver - last - ing   peace!   Sure   as   Je - ho - vah's   Name;   'Tis
3. The   clouds   may   come   and   go,   And   storms   may   sweep   my   sky   This
4. My   love   is   oft - times   low,   My   joy   still   ebbs   and   flows;   But
5. I   change, He   chan - ges   not,   The   Christ   can   ne - ver   die;   His

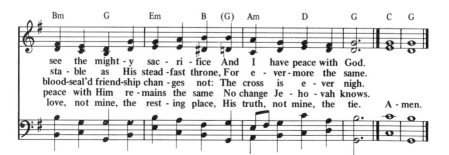

see   the   might - y   sac - ri - fice   And   I   have peace with   God.
sta - ble   as   His   stead - fast   throne,   For   e - ver - more   the   same.
blood - seal'd   friend - ship chan - ges   not: The   cross   is   e - ver   nigh.
peace   with   Him   re - mains   the   same   No change Je - ho - vah   knows.
love,   not   mine,   the   rest - ing   place,   His   truth,   not   mine,   the   tie.   A - men.

103 Children of the Heavenly Father

Faith

As a father pities his children, so the LORD pities/Ps 103:13

Lina Sandell (1832-1903)
tr Ernst Olsen (1870-1958)

Swedish Melody (1874)
arr Marc Hedlin (1942-   )
Tryggare Kan Ingen Vara   8 8 8 8

1. Chil - dren of the heav'n - ly Fa - ther Safe - ly
2. God his own doth tend and nour - ish, In his
3. Nei - ther life nor death shall e - ver From the
4. Praise the Lord in joy - ful num - bers, Your Pro -
5. Though he giv - eth or he tak - eth, God his
6. More se - cure is no one e - ver Than the

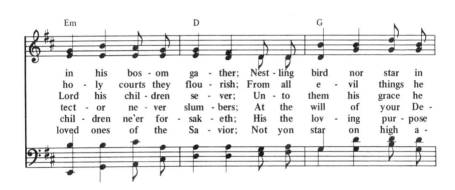

in his bos - om ga - ther; Nest - ling bird nor star in
ho - ly courts they flou - rish; From all e - vil things he
Lord his chil - dren se - ver; Un - to them his grace he
tect - or ne' - ver slum - bers; His the lov - ing pur - pose
chil - dren ne'er for - sak - eth; His the lov - ing pur - pose
loved ones of the Sa - vior; Not yon star on high a -

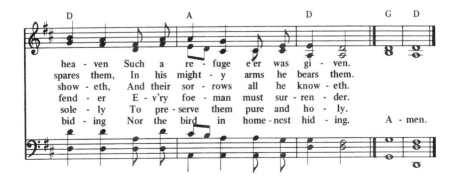

hea - ven Such a re - fuge e'er was gi - ven.
spares them, In his might - y arms he bears them.
show - eth, And their sor - rows all he know - eth.
fend - er E - v'ry foe - man must sur - ren - der.
sole - ly To pre - serve them pure and ho - ly.
bid - ing Nor the bird in home - nest hid - ing.   A - men.

from the Lutheran Service Book and Hymnal *by permission of Fortress Press, 2900 Queen Lane, Philadelphia, PA 19129; arrangement:* © *1976 Marc Hedlin, assigned to Inter-Varsity Christian Fellowship.*

104 Amazing Grace

Faith

And God is able to provide you with every blessing in abundance/2 Cor 9:8

John Newton (1725-1807)
stanza 6 Anon

Traditional American Melody
"Virginia Harmony" (1831)
Amazing Grace 8 6 8 6

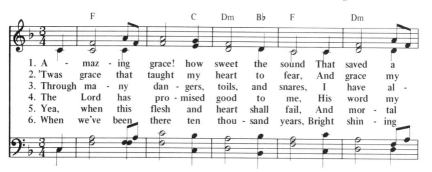

1. A - maz - ing grace! how sweet the sound That saved a
2. 'Twas grace that taught my heart to fear, And grace my
3. Through ma - ny dan - gers, toils, and snares, I have al -
4. The Lord has pro - mised good to me, His word my
5. Yea, when this flesh and heart shall fail, And mor - tal
6. When we've been there ten thou - sand years, Bright shin - ing

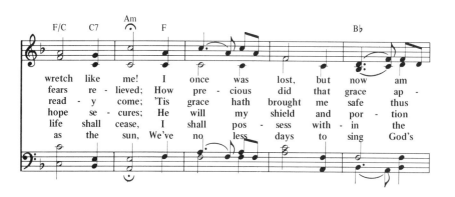

wretch like me! I once was lost, but now am
fears re - lieved; How pre - cious did that grace ap -
read - y come; 'Tis grace hath brought me safe thus
hope se - cures; He will my shield and por - tion
life shall cease, I shall pos - sess with - in the
as the sun, We've no less days to sing God's

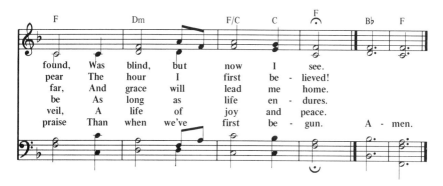

found, Was blind, but now I see.
pear The hour I first be - lieved!
far, And grace will lead me home.
be As long as life en - dures.
veil, A life of joy and peace.
praise Than when we've first be - gun. A - men.

105 Thou Wilt Keep Him in Perfect Peace

Faith

Thou dost keep him in perfect peace, whose mind is stayed on thee/Is 26:3

Scripture

Robert Witty
arr Paul Beckwith (1905-1975)
Furchte Dich Nicht 8 8 8 6

106 Loved with Everlasting Love

[nothing] . . . will be able to separate us from the love of God/Rom 8:38

George W Robinson (1834-1877)

James Mountain (1844-1933)
Everlasting Love 7 7 7 7 D

1. Loved with e - ver - last - ing love, Led by grace that love to know;
2. Heav'n a - bove is soft - er blue, Earth a - round is sweet - er green!
3. Things that once were wild a - larms Can - not now dis - turb my rest;
4. His for - e - ver, on - ly His; Who the Lord and me shall part?

Spi - rit, breath - ing from a - bove, Thou hast taught me it is so!
Some - thing lives in e - v'ry hue Christ - less eyes have ne - ver seen:
Closed in e - ver - last - ing arms, Pil - lowed on the lov - ing breast.
Ah, with what a rest of bliss, Christ can fill the lov - ing heart!

Oh, this full and per - fect peace! Oh, this trans - port all di - vine!
Birds with glad - der songs o'er - flow Flow'rs with deep - er beau - ties shine,
Oh, to lie for - e - ver here, Doubt, and care, and self re - sign,
Heav'n and earth may fade and flee, First born light in gloom de - cline;

In a love which can - not cease, I am His, and He is mine.
Since I know, as now I know, I am His, and He is mine.
While He whis - pers in my ear— I am His, and He is mine.
But while God and I shall be, I am His, and He is mine. A - men.

Come to me, all who labor . . . and I will give you rest/Mt 11:28

Horatius Bonar (1808-1889)

John B Dykes (1823-1876)
Vox Dilecti 8 6 8 6 D

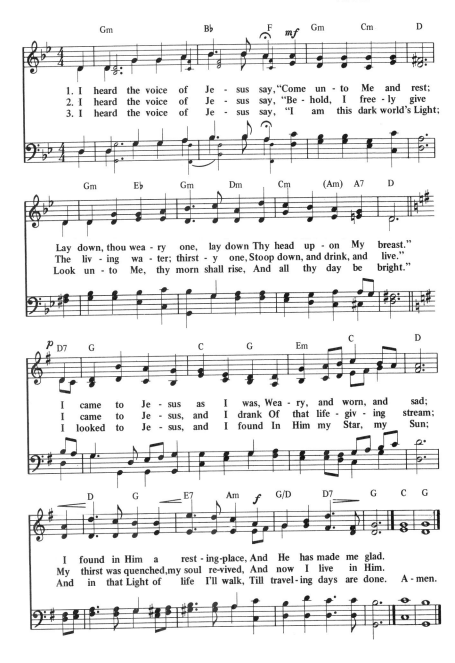

1. I heard the voice of Je - sus say, "Come un - to Me and rest;
2. I heard the voice of Je - sus say, "Be - hold, I free - ly give
3. I heard the voice of Je - sus say, "I am this dark world's Light;

Lay down, thou wea - ry one, lay down Thy head up - on My breast."
The liv - ing wa - ter; thirst - y one, Stoop down, and drink, and live."
Look un - to Me, thy morn shall rise, And all thy day be bright."

I came to Je - sus as I was, Wea - ry, and worn, and sad;
I came to Je - sus, and I drank Of that life - giv - ing stream;
I looked to Je - sus, and I found In Him my Star, my Sun;

I found in Him a rest - ing-place, And He has made me glad.
My thirst was quenched, my soul re - vived, And now I live in Him.
And in that Light of life I'll walk, Till travel - ing days are done. A - men.

108 Jesus, My Lord, My God, My All

Commitment

Whom have I in heaven but thee?/Ps 73:25

Henry Collins (1827-1919)

Hughes M Huffman (1942-   )
Sarah 8 8 8 8 8 8

1. Je - sus, my Lord, my God, my All, Hear me, blest Sa - vior,
2. Je - sus, too late I Thee have sought; How can I love Thee
3. Je - sus, what did Thou find in me That Thou has dealt so
4. Je - sus, of Thee shall be my song; To Thee my heart and

when I call; Hear me, and from Thy dwel - ling - place
as I ought? And how ex - tol Thy match - less fame,
lov - ing - ly? How great the joy that Thou has brought,
soul be - long; All that I have or am is Thine,

Pour down the rich - es of Thy grace:
The glo - rious beau - ty of Thy name?
So far ex - ceed - ing hope or thought! Je - sus, my Lord, I
And Thou, blest Sa - vior, Thou art mine:

Thee a - dore; O make me love Thee more and more. A - men.

109 All for Jesus

Commitment

... present your bodies as a living sacrifice/Rom 12:1

Mary D James (1810-1883)

John Stainer (1840-1901)
Wycliff 8 7 8 7

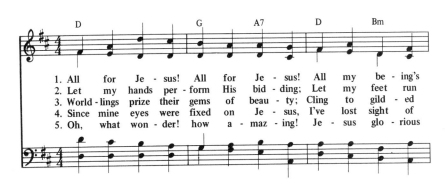

1. All for Je - sus! All for Je - sus! All my be - ing's
2. Let my hands per - form His bid - ding; Let my feet run
3. World - lings prize their gems of beau - ty; Cling to gild - ed
4. Since mine eyes were fixed on Je - sus, I've lost sight of
5. Oh, what won - der! how a - maz - ing! Je - sus glo - rious

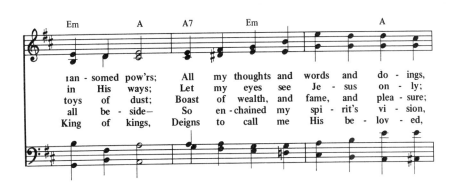

ran - somed pow'rs; All my thoughts and words and do - ings,
in His ways; Let my eyes see Je - sus on - ly;
toys of dust; Boast of wealth, and fame, and plea - sure;
all be - side— So en - chained my spi - rit's vi - sion,
King of kings, Deigns to call me His be - lov - ed,

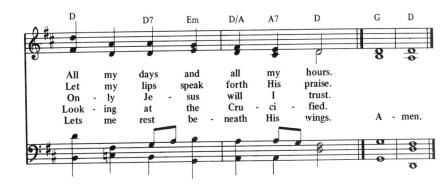

All my days and all my hours.
Let my lips speak forth His praise.
On - ly Je - sus will I trust.
Look - ing at the Cru - ci - fied.
Lets me rest be - neath His wings. A - men.

110 I Am the Lord's!

Commitment

I am my beloved's, and his desire is for me/Song 7:10

Lucy A Bennett (1850-1927)

Joseph Barnby (1838-1896)
Sandringham   11 10 11 10

1. I am the Lord's! O joy be - yond ex - pres - sion,
2. I am the Lord's! It is the glad con - fes - sion,
3. I am the Lord's! Yet teach me all it mean - eth,
4. I am the Lord's! Yes; bo - dy, soul, and spi - rit,

O sweet res - ponse to voice of love Di - vine;
Where - with the Bride re - calls the hap - py day;
All it in - volves of love and loy - al - ty,
O seal them ir - re - cov - er - a - bly Thine;

Faith's joy - ous "Yes" to the as - sur - ing whis - per,
When love's "I will" ac - cept - ed Him for - e - ver,
Of ho - ly ser - vice, ab - so - lute sur - ren - der,
As Thou, Be - lov - ed, in Thy grace and ful - ness

"Fear not! I have re - deem'd thee; thou art Mine."
"The Lord's," to love, to hon - or and o - bey.
And un - re - served o - be - dience un - to Thee.
For - e - ver and for - e - ver - more art mine.   A - men.

111 O the Bitter Shame and Sorrow

For me to live is Christ/Phil 1:21

Theodore Monod (1836-1921)

Peggy S Palmer (1900-   )
Lydbrook   8 7 8 8 7

1. O the bit - ter shame and sor - row, That a time could e - ver be When I let the Sa - vior's pi - ty Plead in vain, and proud - ly an-swered: All of self, and none of Thee!

2. Yet He found me. I be - held Him Bleed - ing on the ac - cur - sed tree, Heard Him pray: For - give them, Fa - ther! And my wist - ful heart said faint - ly: Some of self, and some of Thee!

3. Day by day His ten - der mer - cy, Heal - ing help - ing, full and free, Sweet and strong, and, ah! so pa - tient, Brought me low - er, while I whis-pered: Less of self, and more of Thee!

4. High - er than the high - est hea - ven, Deep - er than the deep - est sea, Lord, Thy love at last has con - quered; Grant me now my sup - pli - ca - tion: None of self, and all of Thee!

A - men.

112 Take My Life, and Let It Be

Commitment

... a living sacrifice, holy and acceptable to God/Rom 12:1

Frances R Havergal (1836-1879)

Wolfgang A Mozart (1756-1791)
Nottingham 7 7 7 7

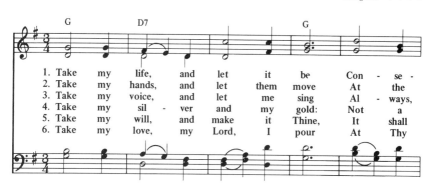

1. Take my life, and let it be Con - se -
2. Take my hands, and let them move At the
3. Take my voice, and let me sing Al - ways,
4. Take my sil - ver and my gold: Not a
5. Take my will, and make it Thine, It shall
6. Take my love, my Lord, I pour At Thy

crat - ed, Lord, to Thee; Take my mo - ments and my
im - pulse of Thy love; Take my feet, and let them
on - ly, for my King; Take my lips, and let them
mite would I with - hold; Take my in - tel - lect, and
be no long - er mine; Take my heart, it is Thine
feet its trea - sure store; Take my - self, and I will

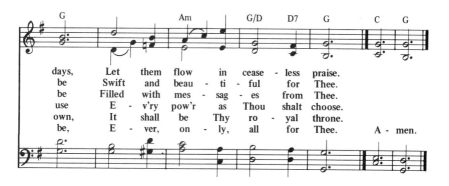

days, Let them flow in cease - less praise.
be Swift and beau - ti - ful for Thee.
be Filled with mes - sag - es from Thee.
use E - v'ry pow'r as Thou shalt choose.
own, It shall be Thy ro - yal throne.
be, E - ver, on - ly, all for Thee. A - men.

113 Lord, in the Fullness of My Might · Commitment

Be strong and of good courage . . . do according to all the law/Jos 1:6-7

Thomas H Gill (1819-1906)

C E Miller (1856-?)
Es Ist Ein Born 8 6 8 6

1. Lord, in the full - ness of my might, I would for Thee be strong;
2. I would not give the world my heart, And then pro - fess Thy love;
3. I would not with swift wing - ed zeal On the world's er - rands go:
4. O not for Thee my weak de - sires, My poor - er bas - er part!
5. O choose me in my gold - en time, In my dear joys have part!

While run - neth o'er each dear de - light, To Thee should soar my song.
I would not feel my strength de - part, And then Thy ser - vice prove.
And la - bor up the heav'n - ly hill With wear - y feet and slow.
O not for Thee my fad - ing fires, The ash - es of my heart.
For Thee the glo - ry of my prime, The full - ness of my heart. A - men.

114 My Glorious Victor, Prince Divine · Commitment

I love my master . . . I will not go out free/Ex 21:5

Handley C G Moule (1841-1920)

R W Dixon
Staincliffe 8 8 8 8

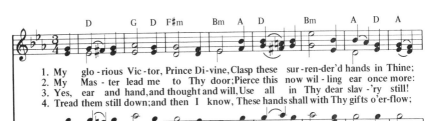

1. My glo - rious Vic - tor, Prince Di - vine, Clasp these sur - ren - der'd hands in Thine;
2. My Mas - ter lead me to Thy door; Pierce this now wil - ling ear once more:
3. Yes, ear and hand, and thought and will, Use all in Thy dear slav - 'ry still!
4. Tread them still down; and then I know, These hands shall with Thy gifts o'er - flow;

At length my will is all Thine own, Glad vas-sal of a Sa-vior's throne.
Thy bonds are free-dom; let me stay With Thee, to toil, en - dure, o - bey.
Self's wea - ry li - ber - ties I cast Be-neath Thy feet; there keep them fast.
And pier-ced ears shall hear the tone Which tells me Thou and I are one. A-men.

115 When I Survey the Wondrous Cross   Commitment

But far be it from me to glory except in the cross/Gal 6:14

Isaac Watts (1674-1748)

Edward Miller (1731-1807)
Rockingham 8 8 8 8

1. When   I   sur - vey   the   won - drous   cross   On   which   the
2. For - bid   it,   Lord,   that   I   should   boast,   Save   in   the
3. See,   from   His   head,   His   hands,   His   feet,   Sor - row   and
4. Were   the   whole   realm   of   na - ture   mine,   That   were   a

Prince   of   glo - ry   died,   My   rich - est   gain   I
death   of   Christ,   my   God;   All   the   vain   things   that
love   flow   min - gled   down;   Did   e'er   such   love   and
pres - ent   far   too   small;   Love   so   a - maz - ing,

count   but   loss,   And   pour   con - tempt   on   all   my   pride.
charm   me   most,   I   sac - ri - fice   them   to   His   blood.
sor - row   meet,   Or   thorns   com - pose   so   rich   a   crown?
so   di - vine,   De - mands   my   soul,   my   life,   my   all.   A - men.

116 My Hope Is Built on Nothing Less — Commitment

He drew me up ... out of the miry bog, and set my feet upon a rock/Ps 40:2

Edward Mote (1797-1874) and others

Alexander B Smith (1889-1950)
Cotswold 8 8 8 8 8 8

1. My hope is built on no-thing less
2. When dark-ness seems to veil His face,
3. His oath, His co - ve - nant, and blood,
4. When the last trum-pet's voice shall sound,

Than Je - sus' blood and
I rest on His un-
Sup-port me in the
O may I then in

right - eous - ness; No me - rit of my own I claim, But
chang - ing grace; In e - v'ry high and stor - my gale My
whelm - ing flood; When all a - round my soul gives way, He
Him be found, Clothed in His right-eous-ness a - lone, Fault-

whol - ly lean on Je - sus' name.
an - chor holds with - in the veil.
then is all my hope and stay.
less to stand be - fore His throne.

On Christ, the

so - lid Rock, I stand; All oth - er ground is sink-ing sand. A - men.

by courtesy of United Reformed Church in England and Wales.

117 Thee Will I Love, My Strength

Commitment

You shall love the Lord your God with all your heart/Lk 10:27

Johann Scheffler (1624-1677)
tr John Wesley (1703-1791)

Henry Carey (1692-1743)
Surrey 8 8 8 8 8 8

1. Thee will I love, my strength, my tow'r, Thee will I love, my joy, my crown, Thee will I love with all my pow'r In all my works and Thee a - lone, Thee will I love 'til sa - cred fire Fills my whole soul with pure de - sire.

2. I thank Thee un - cre - a - ted Sun That thy bright beams on me have shined; I thank Thee, who hast o - ver - thrown My foes, and healed my wound - ed mind: I thank Thee whose en - liven - ing voice Bids my freed heart in Thee re - joice.

3. Up - hold me in the doubt - ful race, Nor suf - fer me a - gain to stray; Strength - en my feet with stead - y pace Still to press for - ward in Thy way: That all my pow'rs, with all their might, In Thy sole glo - ry may u - nite.

4. Thee will I love, my joy, my crown; Thee will I love, my Lord, my God; Thee will I love, be - neath Thy frown Or smile, Thy scep - tre or Thy rod; What though my flesh and heart de - cay, Thee shall I love in end - less day. A - men.

118 O Jesus, I Have Promised

Commitment

If any one serves me, he must follow me/Jn 12:26

John E Bode (1816-1874)

James W Elliott (1833-1915)
Day of Rest 7 6 7 6 D

1. O Je - sus, I have pro - mised To serve Thee to the end;
2. O! let me feel Thee near me; The world is e - ver near;
3. O Je - sus, Thou hast pro - mised To all who fol - low Thee,
4. O! let me hear Thee speak - ing In ac - cents clear and still,

Be Thou for - e - ver near me, My Mas - ter and my Friend!
I see the sights that daz - zle, The tempt - ing sounds I hear.
That where Thou art in glo - ry There shall Thy ser - vant be;
A - bove the storms of pas - sion, The mur - murs of self - will:

I shall not fear the bat - tle, If Thou art by my side,
My foes are e - ver near me, A - round me and with - in;
And, Je - sus, I have pro - mised To serve Thee to the end;
O! speak to re - as - sure me, To has - ten or con - trol;

Nor wan - der from the path - way, If Thou wilt be my Guide.
But, Je - sus, draw Thou near - er, And shield my soul from sin.
O! give me grace to fol - low My Mas - ter and my Friend!
O! speak, and make me lis - ten, Thou Guard - ian of my soul. A - men.

But for you who fear my name the sun of righteousness shall rise/Mal 4:2

Charles Wesley (1707-1788)

Werner's "Choralbuch" (1815)
Ratisbon 7 7 7 7 7 7

1. Christ, whose glo - ry fills the skies, Christ, the true, the
2. Dark and cheer - less is the morn Un - ac - com - pan -
3. Vi - sit then this soul of mine, Pierce the gloom of

on - ly Light, Sun of Right - eous - ness, a - rise,
ied by Thee; Joy - less is the day's re - turn,
sin and grief; Fill me, ra - dian - cy di - vine,

Tri - umph o'er the shades of night; Day - spring from on
Till thy mer - cy's beams I see, Till they in - ward
Scat - ter all my un - be - lief; More and more thy -

high, be near; Day - star, in my heart ap - pear.
light im - part, Glad my eyes, and warm my heart.
self dis - play, Shin - ing to the per - fect day. A - men.

120 Jesus Christ Is Lord Today

Discipleship

As therefore you received Christ Jesus the Lord, so live in him/Col 2:6

W Keith Weathers (1943-   )

W Keith Weathers (1943-   )
Wheaton New   12 14 14 12

1. Je - sus Christ is Lord to - day.   Walk, then, in His   Way!
2. Christ has reigned from his - t'ry's birth.   Think, then, on His   worth!
3. Je - sus Christ the fu - ture brings.   Give Him e - v'ry - thing!

Guar-dian and in - struc - tor, He   makes our sin - closed   eyes to   see;
As He looked and spoke His Will   heav'n and earth with   sub-stance filled;
In the life that He would give   men find strength and   cause to   live;

He main-tains our hu - man needs   and our in - ner   long - ing heeds;
In His grace He planned to make   all men ho - ly   for His sake;
At His name will e - v'ry knee   bow in praise and   wor-ship free;

Je - sus Christ is Lord to - day.   Walk, then, in His   Way!
Christ has reigned from his - t'ry's birth.   Think, then, on His   worth!
Je - sus Christ, E - ter - nal, Same.   Wor - ship, then, His   Name!

© 1976 W Keith Weathers.

121 O, Teach Me What It Meaneth

Discipleship

Jesus ... who was put to death for our trespasses/Rom 4:25

Lucy A Bennett (1850-1927)

Carole S Streeter (1934-   )
Sanderson 7 6 7 6 D

1. O, teach me what it mean - eth: That cross up - lift - ed high,
2. O, teach me what it mean - eth: That sa - cred crim - son tide,
3. O, teach me what it mean - eth: Thy love be - yond com - pare,
4. O, teach me what it mean - eth: For I am full of sin;
5. O In - fi - nite Re - deem - er! I bring no oth - er plea,

With One, the Man of Sor - rows, Con - demned to bleed and die!
The blood and wa - ter flow - ing From Thine own wound - ed side.
The love that reach - eth deep - er Than depths of self de - spair!
And grace a - lone can reach me, And love a - lone can win.
Be - cause Thou dost in - vite me, I cast my - self on Thee.

O, teach me what it cost Thee To make a sin - ner whole;
Teach me that if none oth - er Had sinned but I a - lone,
Yea, teach me, till there glow - eth In this cold heart of mine
O, teach me, for I need Thee, I have no hope be - side,
Be - cause Thou dost ac - cept me, I love and I a - dore;

And teach me, Sa - vior, teach me The val - ue of a soul.
Yet still, Thy blood, Lord Je - sus, Thine on - ly, must a - tone.
Some fee - ble, pale re - flec - tion Of that pure love of Thine.
The chief of all the sin - ners For whom the Sa - vior died.
Be - cause Thy love con - strain - eth, I'll praise Thee e - ver - more! A - men.

I will give thanks to the LORD with my whole heart/Ps 9:1

Charles Wesley (1707-1788)

James Walch (1837-1901)
Sawley   8 6 8 6

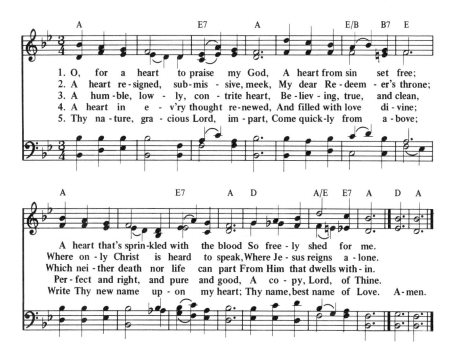

1. O, for a heart to praise my God, A heart from sin set free;
2. A heart re-signed, sub-mis-sive, meek, My dear Re-deem-er's throne;
3. A hum-ble, low-ly, con-trite heart, Be-liev-ing, true, and clean,
4. A heart in e-v'ry thought re-newed, And filled with love di-vine;
5. Thy na-ture, gra-cious Lord, im-part, Come quick-ly from a-bove;

A heart that's sprin-kled with the blood So free-ly shed for me.
Where on-ly Christ is heard to speak, Where Je-sus reigns a-lone.
Which nei-ther death nor life can part From Him that dwells with-in.
Per-fect and right, and pure and good, A co-py, Lord, of Thine.
Write Thy new name up-on my heart; Thy name, best name of Love. A-men.

The grace of the Lord Jesus Christ . . . be with you all/2 Cor 13:14

John Newton (1725-1807)

George C Stebbins (1846-1945)
Sunset   8 7 8 7

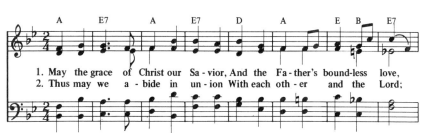

1. May the grace of Christ our Sa-vior, And the Fa-ther's bound-less love,
2. Thus may we a-bide in un-ion With each oth-er and the Lord;

With the Ho - ly Spi - rit's fa - vor, Rest up - on us from a - bove.
And pos - sess, in sweet com - mun - ion, Joys which earth can - not af - ford. A - men.

124 O Jesus Christ, Grow Thou in Me

Discipleship

He must increase, but I must decrease(Jn 3:30

Johann C Lavater (1741-1801)
tr Elizabeth L Smith (1817-1898)

"Henry Greatorex Collection" (1851)
Manoah 8 6 8 6

1. O   Je - sus Christ, grow Thou in me, And   all things else re - cede!
2. Each   day let Thy sup - por -ting might My weak-ness still em-brace;
3. In   Thy bright beams which on me fall, Fade e - v'ry e - vil thought;
4. More   of Thy glo - ry let me see. Thou Ho - ly, wise, and True!
5. Fill   me with glad - ness from a - bove, Hold me by strength Di-vine;
6. Make   this poor self grow less and less, Be   Thou my life and aim;

My heart be dai - ly near - er Thee, From sin be dai - ly freed.
My dark-ness van - ish in Thy light, Thy life my death ef - face.
That I am no -thing, Thou art all, I would be dai - ly taught.
I would Thy liv - ing im - age be, In joy and sor - row too.
Lord, let the glow of Thy great love Through my whole be-ing shine.
O, make me dai - ly through Thy grace, More meet to bear Thy name! A - men.

125 When We Walk with the Lord

If you continue in my word, you are truly my disciples/Jn 8:31

John H Sammis (1846-1919)

Marc Hedlin (1942-   )
Thornhill 6 6 9 D w/refrain

1. When we walk with the Lord / In the light of His Word / What a glo-ry He sheds on our way! / While we do His good will / He a-bides with us still, / And with all who will trust and o-bey.

2. Not a sha-dow can rise, / Not a cloud in the skies, / But His smile quick-ly drives it a-way; / Not a doubt nor a fear, / Not a sigh nor a tear, / Can a-bide while we trust and o-bey.

3. But we ne-ver can prove / The de-lights of His love / Un-til all on the al-tar we lay; / For the fa-vor He shows, / And the joy He be-stows, / Are for them who will trust and o-bey.

4. Then in fel-low-ship sweet / We will sit at His feet, / Or We'll walk by His side in the way; / What He says we will do, / Where He sends we will go, / Ne-ver fear on-ly trust and o-bey.

Trust and o-bey, for there's no oth-er way To be

music: © 1976 Marc Hedlin, assigned to Inter-Varsity Christian Fellowship.

126 May the Mind of Christ My Savior Discipleship

Have this mind among yourselves, which you have in Christ Jesus/Phil 2:5

Kate B Wilkinson (1859-1928)

A Cyril Barham-Gould (1891-1953)
St Leonards 8 7 8 5

1. May the mind of Christ my Sa - vior Live in me from day to day,
2. May the Word of God dwell rich - ly In my heart from hour to hour,
3. May the peace of God my Fa - ther Rule my life in e - v'ry thing,
4. May the love of Je - sus fill me, As the wa - ters fill the sea;
5. May I run the race be - fore me, Strong and brave to face the foe,
6. May His beau - ty rest up - on me As I seek the lost to win,

By His love and pow'r con - trol - ling All I do and say.
So that all may see I tri - umph On - ly thro' His pow'r.
That I may be calm to com - fort Sick and sor - row - ing.
Him ex - alt - ing, self a - bas - ing, This is vic - to - ry.
Look - ing on - ly un - to Je - sus As I on - ward go.
And may they for - get the chan - nel, See - ing on - ly Him. A - men.

words and music: by permission of C Barham-Gould.

127 Teach Me Thy Way, O Lord

Discipleship

Teach me thy way, O LORD; and lead me on a level path/Ps 27:11

B Mansell Ramsey (1849-1923)

B Mansell Ramsey (1849-1923)
Camacha   6 4 6 4 6 6 6 4

1. Teach me Thy Way, O Lord; Teach me Thy Way! Thy guid-ing grace af-ford; Teach me Thy Way! Help me to walk a-right, more by faith less by sight, Lead me with heav'n-ly light; Teach me Thy Way!
2. When I am sad at heart; Teach me Thy Way! When earth-ly joys de-part; Teach me Thy Way! In hours of lone-li-ness, in times of dire dis-tress, In fail-ure or suc-cess, Teach me Thy Way!
3. When doubts and fears a-rise; Teach me Thy Way! When storms o'er spread the skies; Teach me Thy Way! Shine through the cloud and rain, thro' sor-row, toil and pain, Make Thou my path-way plain; Teach me Thy Way!
4. Long as my life shall last; Teach me Thy Way! Wher-e'er my lot be cast; Teach me Thy Way! Un-til the race is run, un-til the jour-ney's done, Un-til the Crown is won; Teach me Thy Way! A-men.

by permission of George Taylor, Stainland, Halifax, England.

128 Guide Me, O Thou Great Jehovah

Guidance

This is God. . . . He will be our guide for ever/Ps 48:14

William Williams (1717-1791)
tr Peter Williams (1722-1796) & others

John Hughes (1873-1932)
Cwm Rhondda 8 7 8 7 8 7 7

1. Guide me, O thou great Je - ho - vah, Pil - grim through this
2. O - pen now the crys - tal foun - tain, Whence the heal - ing
3. When I tread the verge of Jor - dan, Bid my an - xious

bar - ren land; I am weak, but thou art might - y – Hold me
stream doth flow; Let the fire and cloud - y pil - lar Lead me
fears sub - side; Bear me through the swel - ling cur - rent, Land me

with thy pow'r - ful hand: Bread of hea - ven, Bread of hea - ven,
all my jour - ney through: Strong De - liv - 'rer, strong De - liv - 'rer,
safe on Ca - naan's side: Songs of prais - es, songs of prais - es

Feed me till I want no more, Feed me till I want no more.
Be thou still my strength and shield, Be thou still my strength and shield.
I will e - ver give to thee, I will e - ver give to thee. A - men.

129 If Thou but Suffer God to Guide Thee

Guidance

Cast your burden on the LORD, and he will sustain you/Ps 55:22

Georg Neumark (1621-1681)
tr Catherine Winkworth (1827-1878)

Georg Neumark (1621-1681)
Neumark 9 8 9 8 8 8

1. If thou but suf - fer God to guide thee, And hope in
2. O - bey, thou rest - less heart, be still And wait in
3. Sing, pray, and swerve not from His ways; But do thine

Him thro' all thy ways, He'll give the strength, what - e'er be - tide thee,
cheer - ful hope, con - tent To take what - e'er His gra - cious will,
own part faith - ful - ly. Trust His rich pro - mis - es of grace,

And bear thee thro the e - vil days; Who trusts in God's un -
His all dis - cern - ing love, hath sent; Nor doubt our in - most
So shall they be ful - filled in thee. God ne - ver yet for -

chang - ing love Builds on the rock that naught can move.
wants are known To Him who chose us for His own.
sook in need The soul that trust - ed Him in - deed. A - men.

130 Still Will We Trust

Guidance

Trust in the LORD for ever/Is 26:4

William H Burleigh (1812-1871)

Friedrich F Flemming (1778-1813)
Flemming 11 11 11 6

1. Still will we trust, though earth seem dark and drea - ry, And the heart faint be - neath His cha-st'ning rod; Though rough and steep our path - way, worn and wea - ry, Still will we trust in God.

2. Our eyes see dim - ly 'til by faith a - noint - ed, And our blind choos - ing brings us grief and pain; Through Him a - lone, who hath our way ap - point - ed, We find our peace a - gain.

3. Choose for us, God, nor let our weak pre - fer - ring Cheat us of good Thou hast for us de - signed: Choose for us, God; Thy wis - dom is un - err - ing, And we are fools and blind.

4. Let us press on, in pa - tient self de - ni - al, Ac - cept the hard - ship, shrink not from the loss: Our por - tion lies be - yond the hour of tri - al, Our crown be - yond the cross. A - men.

131 Take Thou My Hands and Lead Me

Guidance

...for he has prepared for them a city/Heb 11:16

Julia Hausmann (1825-1901)
tr Martha D Lange

Friedrich Silcher (1789-1860)
So Nimm Denn Meine Hände 7 4 7 4 D

1. Take Thou my hands and lead me A - long life's way, Un -
2. With - in Thy grace so ten - der I would a - bide. Thy
3. I may not glimpse Thy foot - prints, Nor feel Thy pow'r, Yet

til earth's night is ban - ished By ra - diant day. I
per - fect peace my por - tion What - e'er be - tide. I
Thou dost draw me goal - ward Tho' dark the hour. Then,

would not take a sin - gle step A - part from Thee; Where
kneel, dear Lord, be - fore Thee, Be - liev - ing - ly. Thy
take my hands and lead me, Thro' storm - swept night, Till

Thou dost walk or tar - ry, There let me be.
help - less child would trust Though it can - not see.
earth's de - vious ways have end - ed. In heav'ns pure de - light. A - men.

132 Through the Love of God Our Savior

Guidance

. . . in everything God works for good with those who love him/Rom 8:28

Mary Peters (1813-1856)

Welsh Melody
Ar Hyd Y Nos 8 4 8 4 8 8 8 4

1. Through the love of God our Sa - vior, All will be well;
2. Though we pass through tri - bu - la - tion, All will be well;
3. We ex - pect a bright to - mor - row, All will be well;

Free and change-less is His fa - vor, All, all is well;
Ours is such a full sal - va - tion, All, all is well;
Faith can sing, through days of sor - row, All, all is well;

Pre-cious is the blood that heal'd us, Per - fect is the grace that seal'd us,
Hap - py, still in God con - fid - ing, Fruit - ful, if in Christ a - bid - ing
On our Fa - ther's love re - ly - ing, Je - sus e - v'ry need sup - ply - ing,

Strong the hand stretch'd out to shield us, All must be well.
Ho - ly, through the Spi - rit's guid - ing, All must be well.
Or in liv - ing or in dy - ing, All must be well. A - men.

133 Christian, Do You See Them?

Conflict

Resist him, firm in your faith/1 Pet 5:9

Andrew of Crete (d c 740)
tr John M Neale (1818-1866)

John B Dykes (1823-1876)
St Andrew of Crete   6 5 6 5 D

1. Chris-tian, do you see them On the ho-ly ground,
   How the pow'rs of dark - ness Com-pass you a-round?
   Chris-tian, up and smite them, Count-ing gain but loss;
   Smite them, Christ is with you, Sol-dier of the Cross.

2. Chris-tian, do you feel them, How they work with - in,
   Striv-ing, temp-ting, lur - ing, Goad-ing in-to sin?
   Chris-tian, ne - ver trem - ble; Ne - ver be down - cast;
   Gird your-self for bat - tle, Watch, and pray and fast.

3. Chris-tian, do you hear them, How they speak so fair?
   "Quit your wea - ry vi - gil, Cease from watch and prayer."
   Chris-tian, an - swer bold - ly, "While I breathe I pray;"
   Peace shall fol - low bat - tle, Night shall end in day.

4. "Well I know your trou - ble, O my ser - vant true;
   You are ve - ry wea - ry, I was wea - ry too;
   But this toil shall make you Some day all mine own,
   And the end of sor - row Shall be near my throne."

134 Fight the Good Fight with All Thy Might

Conflict

Fight the good fight of the faith/1 Tim 6:12

John S B Monsell (1811-1875)

William Boyd (1847-1928)
Pentecost 8 8 8 8

1. Fight the good fight with all thy might! Christ is thy
2. Run the straight race thro' God's good grace, Lift up thine
3. Cast care a - side, lean on thy Guide, His bound - less
4. Faint not nor fear, His arms are near, He chang - eth

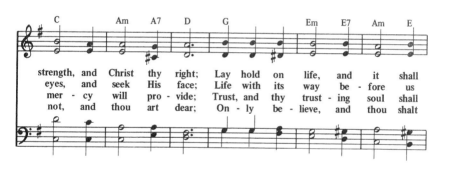

strength, and Christ thy right; Lay hold on life, and it shall
eyes, and seek His face; Life with its way be - fore us
mer - cy will pro - vide; Trust, and thy trust - ing soul shall
not, and thou art dear; On - ly be - lieve, and thou shalt

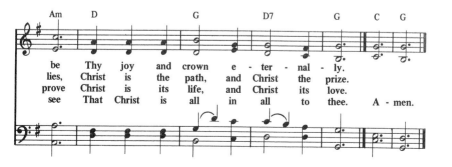

be Thy joy and crown e - ter - nal - ly.
lies, Christ is the path, and Christ the prize.
prove Christ is its life, and Christ its love.
see That Christ is all in all to thee. A - men.

135 Who Is on the Lord's Side?

Conflict

Who is on the LORD's side?/Ex 32:26

Frances R Havergal (1836-1879)

Caradog Roberts (1897-1935)
Rachie 6 5 6 5 D w/refrain

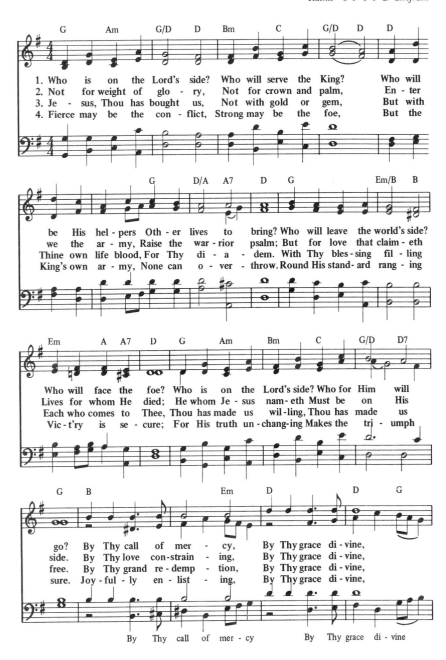

1. Who is on the Lord's side? Who will serve the King? Who will be His helpers Oth-er lives to bring? Who will leave the world's side? Who will face the foe? Who is on the Lord's side? Who for Him will go? By Thy call of mer - cy, By Thy grace di - vine,

2. Not for weight of glo - ry, Not for crown and palm, En - ter we the ar - my, Raise the war - rior psalm; But for love that claim - eth Lives for whom He died; He whom Je - sus nam - eth Must be on His side. By Thy love con-strain - ing, By Thy grace di - vine,

3. Je - sus, Thou has bought us, Not with gold or gem, But with Thine own life blood, For Thy di - a - dem. With Thy bles - sing fil - ling Each who comes to Thee, Thou has made us wil - ling, Thou has made us free. By Thy grand re - demp - tion, By Thy grace di - vine,

4. Fierce may be the con - flict, Strong may be the foe, But the King's own ar - my, None can o - ver - throw. Round His stand-ard rang - ing Vic - t'ry is se - cure; For His truth un -chang-ing Makes the tri - umph sure. Joy - ful - ly en - list - ing, By Thy grace di - vine,

By Thy call of mer - cy By Thy grace di - vine

We are on the Lord's side, Sa-vior, we are Thine. A-men.

136 Why Should I Fear the Darkest Hour   Conflict

I can do all things in him who strengthens me/Phil 4:13

John Newton (1725-1807)

Peggy S Palmer (1900-   )
Keynsham 8 8 8

1. Why should I fear the dark-est hour,   Or trem-ble at the
2. Though hot the fight, why quit the field?   Why must I ei - ther
3. I know not what may soon be-tide,   Or how my wants shall
4. Though sin would fill me with dis - tress,   The throne of grace I
5. Though faint my prayers and cold my love,   My stead-fast hope shall
6. A - gainst me earth and hell com - bine;   But on my side is

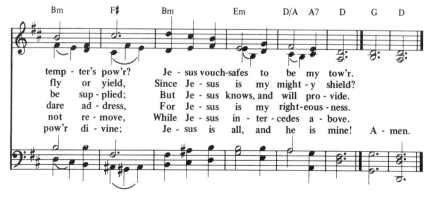

temp - ter's pow'r?   Je - sus vouch-safes to be my tow'r.
fly or yield,   Since Je - sus is my might - y shield?
be sup-plied;   But Je - sus knows, and will pro - vide.
dare ad - dress,   For Je - sus is my right-eous - ness.
not re - move,   While Je - sus in - ter-cedes a - bove.
pow'r di - vine;   Je - sus is all, and he is mine!   A - men.

137 Peace, Perfect Peace

Thou dost keep him in perfect peace, whose mind is stayed on thee/Is 26:3

Edward H Bickersteth (1825-1906)

William H Jude (1851-1922)
10 10

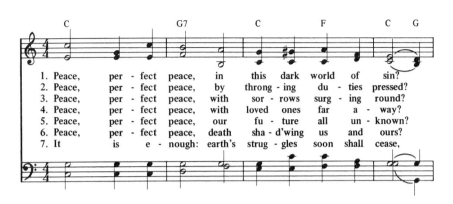

1. Peace, per - fect peace, in this dark world of sin?
2. Peace, per - fect peace, by throng - ing du - ties pressed?
3. Peace, per - fect peace, with sor - rows surg - ing round?
4. Peace, per - fect peace, with loved ones far a - way?
5. Peace, per - fect peace, our fu - ture all un - known?
6. Peace, per - fect peace, death sha - d'wing us and ours?
7. It is e - nough: earth's strug - gles soon shall cease,

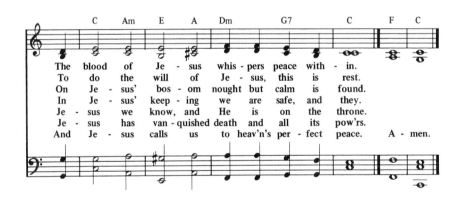

The blood of Je - sus whis - pers peace with - in.
To do the will of Je - sus, this is rest.
On Je - sus' bos - om nought but calm is found.
In Je - sus' keep - ing we are safe, and they.
Je - sus we know, and He is on the throne.
Je - sus has van - quished death and all its pow'rs.
And Je - sus calls us to heav'n's per - fect peace. A - men.

138 Come, My Soul, Thy Suit Prepare

Prayer

Ask, and it will be given you/Mt 7:7

John Newton (1725-1807)

Xavier Schnyder (1786-1868)
Horton 7 7 7 7

1. Come, my soul, thy suit pre - pare: Je - sus
2. Thou art com - ing to a King, Large pe -
3. With my bur - den I be - gin: Lord, re -
4. Lord, I come to Thee for rest, Take pos -
5. While I am a pil - grim here, Let Thy
6. Show me what I have to do, E - v'ry

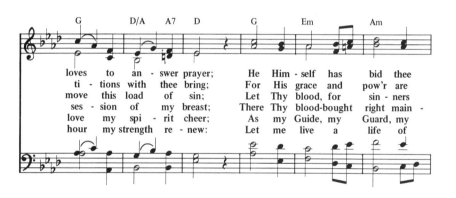

loves to an - swer prayer; He Him - self has bid thee
ti - tions with thee bring; For His grace and pow'r are
move this load of sin; Let Thy blood, for sin - ners
ses - sion of my breast; There Thy blood-bought right main -
love my spi - rit cheer; As my Guide, my Guard, my
hour my strength re - new: Let me live a life of

pray, There - fore will not say thee nay.
such, None can e - ver ask too much.
spilt, Set my con - science free from guilt.
tain, And with - out a ri - val reign.
Friend, Lead me to my jour - ney's end.
faith, Let me die Thy peo - ple's death. A - men.

139 What a Friend We Have in Jesus

For the eyes of the Lord are upon the righteous/1 Pet 3:12

Joseph M Scriven (1820-1886)

William P Rowlands (1860-1937)
Blaenwern   8 7 8 7 D

1. What a Friend we have in Je - sus, All our sins and griefs to bear! What a pri - vi - lege to car - ry E - v'ry-thing to God in prayer! O what peace we of - ten for - feit, O what need - less pain we bear, All be - cause we

2. Have we tri - als and temp - ta - tions? Is there trou - ble an - y - where? We should ne - ver be dis - cou - raged: Take it to the Lord in prayer. Can we find a friend so faith - ful, Who will all our sor - rows share? Je - sus knows our

3. Are we weak and hea - vy - la - den, Cum - bered with a load of care? Je - sus on - ly is our re - fuge: Take it to the Lord in prayer. Do thy friends des - pise, for - sake thee? Take it to the Lord in prayer; In His arms He'll

do not car - ry E - v'ry - thing to God in prayer!
e - v'ry weak - ness: Take it to the Lord in prayer.
take and shield thee! Thou wilt find a so - lace there. A - men.

music: by permission of Mr Glyn A Gabe, Langland, Swansea, S. Wales.

140 Speak, Lord, in the Stillness

Prayer

Speak, LORD, for thy servant hears/1 Sam 3:9

E May Grimes (1868-1927)

Harold Green (1871-1931)
Quietude 6 5 6 5

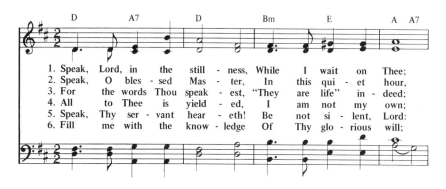

1. Speak, Lord, in the still - ness, While I wait on Thee;
2. Speak, O bles - sed Mas - ter, In this qui - et hour,
3. For the words Thou speak - est, "They are life" in - deed;
4. All to Thee is yield - ed, I am not my own;
5. Speak, Thy ser - vant hear - eth! Be not si - lent, Lord:
6. Fill me with the know - ledge Of Thy glo - rious will;

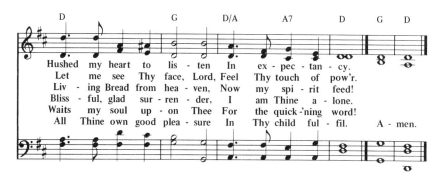

Hushed my heart to lis - ten In ex - pec - tan - cy.
Let me see Thy face, Lord, Feel Thy touch of pow'r.
Liv - ing Bread from hea - ven, Now my spi - rit feed!
Bliss - ful, glad sur - ren - der, I am Thine a - lone.
Waits my soul up - on Thee For the quick - 'ning word!
All Thine own good plea - sure In Thy child ful - fil. A - men.

used by permission of the Africa Evangelical Fellowship/SAGM, London.

141 Approach, My Soul, the Mercy-Seat

Prayer

Let us then with confidence draw near to the throne of grace/Heb 4:16

John Newton (1725-1807)

Charles Hutcheson (1792-1860)
Stracathro   8 6 8 6

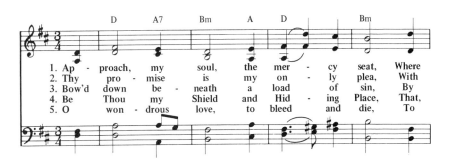

1. Ap - proach, my soul, the mer - cy seat, Where
2. Thy pro - mise is my on - ly plea, With
3. Bow'd down be - neath a load of sin, By
4. Be Thou my Shield and Hid - ing Place, That,
5. O won - drous love, to bleed and die, To

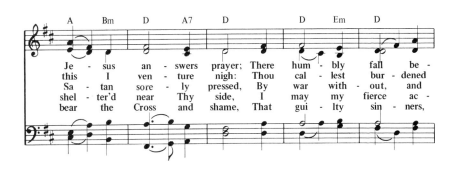

Je - sus an - swers prayer; There hum - bly fall be -
this I ven - ture nigh: Thou cal - lest bur - dened
Sa - tan sore - ly pressed, By war with - out, and
shel - ter'd near Thy side, I may my fierce ac -
bear the Cross and shame, That gui - lty sin - ners,

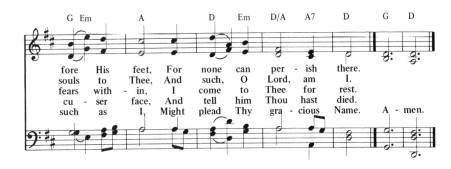

fore His feet, For none can per - ish there.
souls to Thee, And such, O Lord, am I.
fears with - in, I come to Thee for rest.
cu - ser face, And tell him Thou hast died.
such as I, Might plead Thy gra - cious Name. A - men.

142 Let Us, with a Gladsome Mind

Thankfulness

O give thanks to the LORD, for he is good/Ps 136:1

John Milton (1608-1674)

John Antes (1740-1811)
arr John B Wilkes (1785-1869)
Monkland 7 7 7 7

1. Let us, with a glad - some mind, Praise the Lord for He is kind:
2. Let us sound His Name a - broad, For of gods He is the God:
3. He with all - com - mand - ing might Filled the new - made world with light:
4. All things liv - ing He doth feed; His full hand sup - plies their need:
5. Let us then with glad - some mind, Praise the Lord for He is kind:

For His mer - cies shall en - dure, E - ver - faith - ful, e - ver - sure. A - men.

143 Be Present at Our Table, Lord

Thankfulness

God is love/1 Jn 4:16

Anon

Anon
Mercy's Free 8 6 8 6 8 8 8 6

Be pres - ent at our ta - ble, Lord; God is love, God is love,
Be here and e - v'ry where a - dored; God is love, God is love.

These mer - cies bless and grant that we may live in fel - low - ship with Thee,

May live in fel - low - ship with Thee God is love, God is love.

144 We Plow the Fields and Scatter

Thankfulness

... every perfect gift is from above/Jas 1:17

Malthias Claudius (1740-1815)
tr Jane M Campbell (1817-1878)

Johann A P Schulz (1747-1800)
Wir Pflügen 7 6 7 6 D w/refrain

1. We plow the fields and scat - ter The good seed on the land,
2. He on - ly is the ma - ker Of all things near and far,
3. We thank thee, then, O Fa - ther, For all things bright and good—

But it is fed and wa - tered By God's al - might - y hand;
He paints the way - side flow - er, He lights the eve - ning star;
The seed - time and the har - vest, Our life, our health, our food;

He sends the snow in win - ter, The warmth to swell the grain,
The winds and waves o - bey him, By him the birds are fed:
No gifts have we to of - fer For all thy love im - parts,

The breez - es and the sun - shine, And soft, re - fresh - ing rain.
Much more, to us his chil - dren, He gives our dai - ly bread.
But that which Thou de - sir - est, Our hum - ble, thank - ful hearts.

All good gifts a-round us Are sent from heav'n a-bove:

Then thank the Lord, O thank the Lord For all his love. A - men.

145 How Good Is the God We Adore

Thankfulness

The LORD is good to all, and his compassion is over all/Ps 145:9

Joseph Hart (1712-1768)

"Lancashire Sunday-School Songs" (1657)
Celeste 8 8 8 8

1. How good is the God we a - dore, Our faith - ful un - change - a - ble Friend!
2. 'Tis Je - sus the First and the Last, Whose Spi - rit shall guide us safe home;

His love is as great as His pow'r, And knows nei-ther mea-sure nor end!
We'll praise Him for all that is past, And trust Him for all that's to come. A - men.

146 My God, I Thank Thee

Thankfulness

. . . we also rejoice in God through our Lord Jesus Christ/Rom 5:11

Adelaide A Proctor (1825-1864)

Frederick C Maker (1844-1927)
Wentworth 8 4 8 4 8 4

1. My God, I thank Thee, who hast made The earth so bright,
2. I thank Thee, too, that Thou hast made Joy to a - bound,
3. I thank Thee more, that all our joy Is touched with pain,
4. For Thou, who know - est, Lord, how soon Our weak heart clings,
5. I thank Thee, Lord, that here our souls, Though am - ply blest,

So full of splen - dor and of joy, beau - ty and light;
So ma - ny gen - tle thoughts and deeds cir - cling us round,
That sha - dows fall on bright - est hours That thorns re - main,
Hast given us joys, ten - der and true, Yet all with wings,
Can ne - ver find, al - though they seek, A per - fect rest,

So ma - ny glo - rious things are here, No - ble and right.
That in the dark - est spot of earth Some love is found.
So that earth's bliss may be our guide, and not our chain.
So that we see, gleam - ing on high, Di - vi - ner things.
Nor e - ver shall, un - til they lean On Je - sus' breast. A - men.

by kind permission of Psalms & Hymns Trust, London.

147 For Thy Daily Mercies

Thankfulness

I will sing aloud of thy steadfast love/Ps 59:16

Frank Houghton (1894-1972)

Kenneth G Finlay (1882-   )
Glenfinlas 6 5 11

For Thy dai - ly mer - cies Be Thy Name a - dored!

More than all we praise Thee for Thy - self, O Lord! A - men.

words: by permission of Mrs Frank Houghton; music: by permission of Broomhill Church of Scotland as beneficiaries under the will of the late Kenneth George Finlay.

148 Now Thank We All Our God

Thankfulness

And now we thank thee, our God, and praise thy glorious name/1 Chron 29:13

Martin Rinkart (1586-1649)
tr Catherine Winkworth (1827-1878)

Johann Crüger (1598-1662)
Nun Danket 6 7 6 7 6 6 6 6

1. Now thank we all our God With heart and hands and voic - es,
2. O may this boun-teous God Through all our life be near us,
3. All praise and thanks to God The Fa - ther now be giv - en,

Who won-drous things hath done, In whom His world re - joic - es;
With e - ver joy - ful hearts And bles - sed peace to cheer us;
The Son, and Him who reigns With them in high - est hea - ven,

Who, from our moth - er's arms, Hath blessed us on our way
And keep us in His grace And guide us when per - plexed,
The one e - ter - nal God Whom earth and heav'n a - dore;

With count-less gifts of love, And still is ours to - day.
And free us from all ills In this world and the next.
For thus it was, is now, And shall be e - ver - more. A - men.

149 Cedar Grace

Thankfulness

Thou dost cause . . . bread to strengthen man's heart/Ps 104:14, 15

W J Martin

Jean Sibelius (1865-1957)
Finlandia 11 10 11 10 11 10

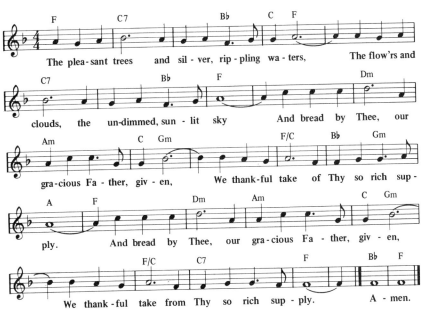

The plea-sant trees and sil - ver, rip-pling wa - ters, The flow'rs and clouds, the un-dimmed, sun - lit sky And bread by Thee, our gra-cious Fa - ther, giv - en, We thank-ful take of Thy so rich sup - ply. And bread by Thee, our gra-cious Fa - ther, giv - en, We thank-ful take from Thy so rich sup - ply. A - men.

words: © 1960 by Inter-Varsity Christian Fellowship; melody: "Finlandia" by Jean Sibelius. Used by permission of Breitkopf & Härtel, Wiesbaden.

150 We Thank Thee, Lord

Thankfulness

. . . always and for everything giving thanks/Eph 5:20

C.I.M. Grace
Anon

Cuthbert Howard (1856-1927)
Lloyd 8 6 8 6

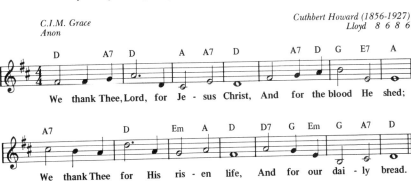

We thank Thee, Lord, for Je - sus Christ, And for the blood He shed; We thank Thee for His ris - en life, And for our dai - ly bread.

tune: by permission of George Taylor, Stainland, Halifax, England.

151 Give, O Give Thanks to the Lord!

Thankfulness

O give thanks to the LORD . . . for his steadfast love endures for ever/Ps 136:1

Anon

German Canon
6 6 6 5

Give, O give, thanks to the Lord! For He is so faith - ful,
Rend - ons grâces au Seign - eur, Il est char - i - ta - ble,
Dan - ket, dan - ket dem Herrn denn Er ist so freund - lich,

And His truth and good - ness, They shall ne - ver end.
Sa bon - té, sa veri - té, Durent pour l'é-ter - ni - té!
Sei - ne Güt' und Wahr - heit Wäh - ret e - wig - lich.

English translation © 1960 Inter-Varsity Christian Fellowship.

152 Gelobet Sei*

Thankfulness

I will sing praise to the name of the LORD/Ps 7:17

Anon

German Round
Gelobet Sei 8 4 8 4 6 8
*"praises be to the Lord my God"

Ge - lo - bet sei, ge - lo - bet sei

der Herr mein Gott! Ge - lo - bet sei, ge -

lo - bet sei der Herr mein Gott! Ge - lo - bet, ge -

lo - bet, ge - lo - bet sei der Herr mein Gott.

Scriptures

How I love Thy law, O Lord!
Daily joy its truths afford;
In its constant light I go,
Wise to conquer every foe.
Sweeter are Thy words to me
Than all other good can be;
Safe I walk, Thy truth my light,
Hating falsehood, loving right.
Psalm 119

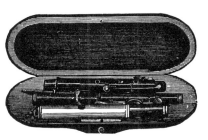

153 How Firm a Foundation

The Scriptures

Heaven and earth will pass away, but my words will not pass away/Lk 21:33

Rippon's "Selection of Hymns" (1787)

Traditional American Melody
Caldwell's "Union Harmony" (1837)
Foundation 11 11 11 11

1. How firm a foun - da - tion, ye saints of the Lord,
2. "Fear not, I am with thee, O be not dis - mayed,
3. "When through the deep wa - ters I call thee to go,
4. "When through fier - y tri - als thy path - way shall lie,
5. "The soul that on Je - sus hath leaned for re - pose,

Is laid for your faith in His ex - cel - lent word!
For I am thy God, and will still give thee aid;
The riv - ers of sor - row shall not o - ver - flow;
My grace, all - suf - fi - cient, shall be thy sup - ply;
I will not, I will not de - sert to his foes;

What more can He say than to you He hath said,
I'll strength - en thee, help thee, and cause thee to stand,
For I will be with thee, thy trou - bles to bless,
The flame shall not hurt thee; I on - ly de - sign
That soul, though all hell should en - dea - vor to shake,

To you who for re - fuge to Je - sus have fled.
Up - held by My right - eous, om - ni - po - tent hand.
And sanc - ti - fy to thee thy deep - est dis - tress.
Thy dross to con - sume, and thy gold to re - fine.
I'll ne - ver, no ne - ver, no ne - ver for - sake!" A - men.

154 O Word of God Incarnate

The Scriptures

... the sacred writings which ... instruct you for salvation/2 Tim 3:15

William W How (1823-1897)

"Neu-Vermehrtes Gesangbuch" Meiningen (1693)
arr Felix Mendelssohn (1809-1847)
Munich 7 6 7 6 D

1. O Word of God in-car-nate, O Wis-dom from on high,
2. The Church from her dear Mas-ter Re-ceived the gift di-vine,
3. It float-eth like a ban-ner Be-fore God's host un-furled;
4. O make thy Church, dear Sa-vior, A lamp of bur-nished gold,

O Truth un-changed, un-chang-ing, O Light of our dark sky,
And still that light she lift-eth O'er all the earth to shine.
It shin-eth like a bea-con A-bove the dark-ling world.
To bear a-mong the na-tions Thy true light as of old.

We praise thee for the ra-diance That from the hal-lowed page,
It is the gold-en cas-ket Where gems of truth are stored;
It is the chart and com-pass That o'er life's surg-ing sea,
O teach thy wan-d'ring pil-grims By this their path to trace,

A lan-tern to our foot-steps, Shines on from age to age.
It is the heav'n-drawn pic-ture Of Christ, the liv-ing Word.
'Mid mists, and rocks, and quick-sands, Still guides, O Christ, to thee.
Till, clouds and dark-ness end-ed, They see thee face to face! A-men.

155 God, in the Gospel of His Son

The Scriptures

In him . . . who accomplishes all things according to the counsel of his will/Eph 1:11

Benjamin Beddome and
Thomas Cotterill (1779-1823)

Edward Miller (1731-1807)
Rockingham 8 8 8 8

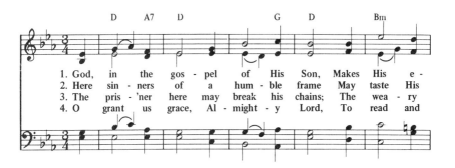

1. God, in the gos - pel of His Son, Makes His e -
2. Here sin - ners of a hum - ble frame May taste His
3. The pris - 'ner here may break his chains; The wea - ry
4. O grant us grace, Al - might - y Lord, To read and

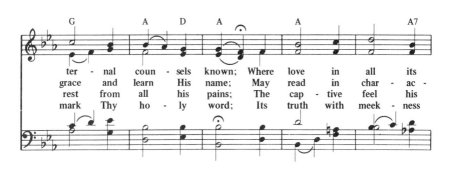

ter - nal coun - sels known; Where love in all its
grace and learn His name; May read in char - ac -
rest from all his pains; The cap - tive feel his
mark Thy ho - ly word; Its truth with meek - ness

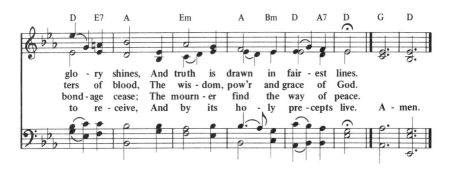

glo - ry shines, And truth is drawn in fair - est lines.
ters of blood, The wis - dom, pow'r and grace of God.
bond - age cease; The mourn - er find the way of peace.
to re - ceive, And by its ho - ly pre - cepts live. A - men.

156 O God of Light, Thy Word
The Scriptures

Thy word is a lamp to my feet and a light to my path/Ps 119:105

Sarah E Taylor (1883-1954)

John B Dykes (1823-1876)
re-harmonized Robin Sheldon (1932-   )
Strength and Stay   11 10 11 10

1. O God of light, thy Word, a lamp un - fail - ing,
2. From days of old, thru swift - ly rol - ling a - ges,
3. Un - dimmed by time, the Word is still re - veal - ing
4. To all the world the mes - sage thou art send - ing,

Shines thru the dark - ness of our earth - ly way,
Thou hast re - vealed thy will to mor - tal men,
To sin - ful men thy jus - tice and thy grace;
To e - v'ry land, to e - v'ry race and clan;

O'er fear and doubt, o'er all des - pair pre - vail - ing,
Speak - ing to saints, to pro - phets, kings, and sa - ges,
And quest - ing hearts that long for peace and heal - ing
And my - riad tongues, in one great an - them blend - ing,

Guid - ing our steps to thine e - ter - nal day.
Who wrote the mes - sage with im - mor - tal pen.
See thy com - pas - sion in the Sa - vior's face.
Ac - claim with joy thy won-drous gift to man. A - men.

157 How I Love Thy Law, O Lord!

The Scriptures

Oh, how I love thy law! It is my meditation all the day/Ps 119:97

Psalm 119

Anon
arr Benjamin Carr (1768-1831)
Spanish Chant 7 7 7 7 w/refrain

1. How I love Thy law, O Lord! Dai - ly joy its truths af - ford;
2. Thy com-mand-ments in my heart Tru - est wis - dom can im - part;
3. While my heart Thy word o - beys, I am kept from e - vil ways;

In its con - stant light I go, Wise to con - quer e - v'ry foe.
To mine eyes Thy pre - cepts show Wis - dom more than sa - ges know.
From Thy law, with Thee to guide, I have ne - ver turned a - side.

Sweet - er are Thy words to me Than all oth - er good can be;

Safe I walk, Thy truth my light, Hat - ing false-hood, lov - ing right. A - men.

Church

Jesus Christ, our sure foundation,
He whose purpose stays the same,
Building for himself a nation,
Giving those He calls His name.
Praise we now and evermore,
Jesus we adore!
God has given to us salvation,
Jesus Christ has borne our blame.

Mark Hunt

158 Glorious Things of Thee Are Spoken

The Church

Glorious things are spoken of you, O city of God/Ps 87:3

John Newton (1725-1807)

Franz J Haydn (1732-1809)
Austrian Hymn 8 7 8 7 D

1. Glo - rious things of thee are spo - ken, Zi - on, ci - ty of our God.
2. See the streams of liv - ing wa - ters, Spring-ing from e - ter - nal love.
3. Round each hab - i - ta - tion hov-ering, See the cloud and fire ap - pear
4. Sa - vior, if of Zi - on's ci - ty, I through grace a mem - ber am,

He whose word can - not be bro - ken Formed thee for His own a - bode;
Well sup - ply thy sons and daugh-ters, And all fear of want re - move:
For a glo - ry and a cov - ering, Show - ing that the Lord is near!
Let the world de - ride or pi - ty, I will glo - ry in Thy name;

On the Rock of A - ges found - ed, What can shake thy sure re - pose?
Who can faint, while such a riv - er E - ver will their thirst as - suage?
Thus de - ri - ving from their ban - ner Light by night and shade by day;
Fad - ing is the world's best plea - sure, All its boast - ed pomp and show;

With sal - va - tion's walls sur-round-ed, Thou mayst smile at all thy foes.
Grace which, like the Lord, the Giv - er, Ne - ver fails from age to age.
Safe they feed up - on the man - na Which He gives them when they pray.
Sol - id joys and last - ing trea - sure None but Zi - on's chil-dren's know. A - men.

159 For All the Saints

The Church

Therefore, since we are surrounded by so great a cloud of witnesses/Heb 12:1

William W How (1823-1897)

Ralph Vaughan Williams (1872-1958)
Sine Nomine 10 10 10 w/Alleluias

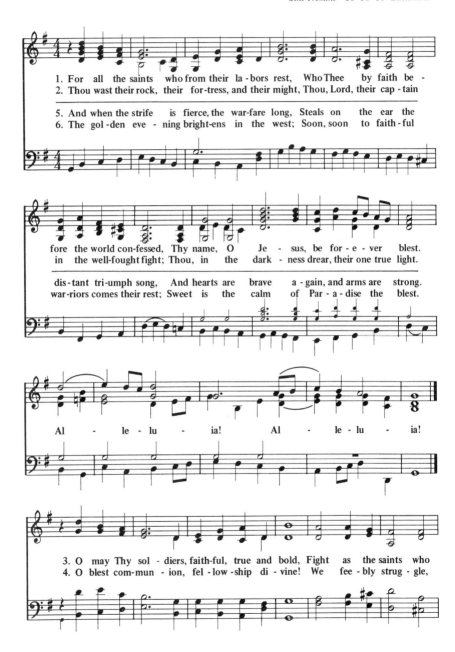

1. For all the saints who from their la-bors rest, Who Thee by faith be-
2. Thou wast their rock, their for-tress, and their might, Thou, Lord, their cap-tain

5. And when the strife is fierce, the war-fare long, Steals on the ear the
6. The gol-den eve-ning bright-ens in the west; Soon, soon to faith-ful

fore the world con-fessed, Thy name, O Je-sus, be for-e-ver blest.
in the well-fought fight; Thou, in the dark-ness drear, their one true light.

dis-tant tri-umph song, And hearts are brave a-gain, and arms are strong.
war-riors comes their rest; Sweet is the calm of Par-a-dise the blest.

Al - le - lu - ia! Al - le - lu - ia!

3. O may Thy sol-diers, faith-ful, true and bold, Fight as the saints who
4. O blest com-mun-ion, fel-low-ship di-vine! We fee-bly strug-gle,

no - bly fought of old, And win with them the vic - tor's crown of gold.
they in glo - ry shine; Yet all are one in Thee, for all are Thine.

Al - le - lu - ia, Al - le - lu - ia!

from the English Hymnal *by permission of Oxford University Press.*

160 **According to Thy Gracious Word** The Church
This do in remembrance of me/Lk 22:19

James Montgomery (1771-1854)

Henry Greatorex (1811-1858)
Manoah 8 6 8 6

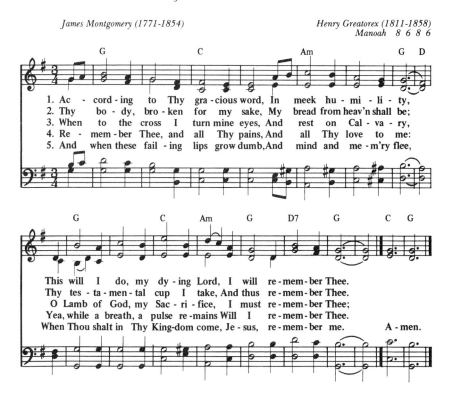

1. Ac - cord - ing to Thy gra - cious word, In meek hu - mi - li - ty,
2. Thy bo - dy, bro - ken for my sake, My bread from heav'n shall be;
3. When to the cross I turn mine eyes, And rest on Cal - va - ry,
4. Re - mem - ber Thee, and all Thy pains, And all Thy love to me:
5. And when these fail - ing lips grow dumb, And mind and me - m'ry flee,

This will I do, my dy - ing Lord, I will re - mem - ber Thee.
Thy tes - ta - men - tal cup I take, And thus re - mem - ber Thee.
O Lamb of God, my Sac - ri - fice, I must re - mem - ber Thee;
Yea, while a breath, a pulse re - mains Will I re - mem - ber Thee.
When Thou shalt in Thy King - dom come, Je - sus, re - mem - ber me. A - men.

161 The Church's One Foundation

The Church

...no other foundation ... than ... Jesus Christ/1 Cor 3:11

Samuel J Stone (1839-1900)

Samuel S Wesley (1810-1876)
Aurelia 7 6 7 6 D

1. The Church-'s one foun-da-tion Is Je-sus Christ her Lord;
2. E-lect from e-v'ry na-tion, Yet one o'er all the earth,
3. 'Mid toil and trib-u-la-tion, And tu-mult of her war,
4. Yet she on earth hath un-ion With God the Three in One,

She is His new cre-a-tion By wa-ter and the word:
Her char-ter of sal-va-tion, One Lord, one faith, one birth;
She waits the con-sum-ma-tion Of peace for e-ver-more;
And mys-tic sweet com-mun-ion With those whose rest is won:

From heav'n He came and sought her To be His ho-ly bride;
One ho-ly Name she bles-ses, Par-takes one ho-ly food,
Till, with the vi-sion glo-rious, Her long-ing eyes are blest,
O hap-py ones and ho-ly! Lord, give us grace that we,

With His own blood He bought her, And for her life He died.
And to one hope she pres-ses, With e-v'ry grace en-dued.
And the great Church vic-to-rious Shall be the Church at rest.
Like them, the meek and low-ly, On high may dwell with Thee. A-men.

162 Jesus Christ Our Sure Foundation

I am laying in Zion for a foundation ... a sure foundation/Is 28:16

Mark Hunt (1951-   )

Hughes M Huffman (1942-   )
Oakbrook 8 7 8 7 7 5 8 7

1. Je - sus Christ, our sure foun - da - tion, He whose pur - pose stays the same,
2. Shep - herd, Guar-dian, he who teach - es, On whose grace the Church de-pends,
3. Je - sus, come, your king-dom bring-ing, How we long to see its sight!

Build - ing for him - self a na - tion, Giv - ing those he calls his name.
Tend - ing it through his-t'ry's reach - es, And will keep it to the end.
E - v'ry saint Christ's prai-ses sing - ing, Stands be - fore th'E - ter - nal Light.

Praise we now and e - ver -more, Je - sus we a - dore! God has
Praise we now and e - ver -more, Je - sus we a - dore! He who
Praise we now and e - ver -more, Je - sus we a - dore! Ex - al -

giv'n to us sal - va - tion, Je - sus Christ has borne our blame.
from the first did seek us, Sa - vior, Ru - ler, Guide and Friend.
ta - tion e - ver ring - ing, Christ, our King, re - turn in might. A - men.

music: © 1970 Hughes M Huffman, assigned to Inter-Varsity Christian Fellowship; words: © 1976 Mark Hunt, assigned to Inter-Varsity Christian Fellowship.

163 He Walks among the Golden Lamps

The Church

... and in the midst of the lampstands one like a son of man/Rev 1:13

Timothy Dudley-Smith

Noel Tredinnick
8 6 8 8 8 6

1. He walks a-mong the gol-den lamps On feet like bur-nished bronze; His hair as snows of win-ter white, His eyes with fire a-flame and bright His glo-rious robe of seam-less light Sur-pas-sing So-lo-mon's.

2. And in His hand the se-ven stars And from His mouth a sword: His voice the thun-der of the seas; All crea-tures bow to His de-crees Who holds the e-ver-last-ing keys And reigns as So-v'reign Lord.

3. More ra-diant than the sun at noon, Who was, and is to be: Who was, from e-ver-last-ing days; Who lives, the Lord of all our ways; To Him be ma-jes-ty and praise For all e-ter-ni-ty.

164 He Walks among the Golden Lamps
The Church

... and in the midst of the lampstands one like a son of man/Rev 1:13

Timothy Dudley-Smith

Norman Warren (1934-   )
8 6 8 8 8 6

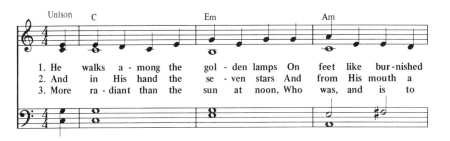

1. He walks a-mong the gol-den lamps On feet like bur-nished
2. And in His hand the se-ven stars And from His mouth a
3. More ra-diant than the sun at noon, Who was, and is to

bronze; His hair as snows of win-ter white, His
sword: His voice the thun-der of the seas; All
be: Who was, from e-ver-last-ing days; Who

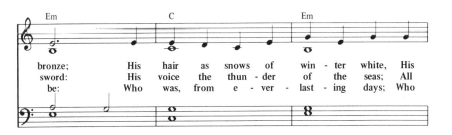

eyes with fire a-flame, and bright His glo-rious robe of
crea-tures bow to His de-crees Who holds the e-ver-
lives, the Lord of all our ways; To Him be ma-jes-

seam-less light Sur-pas-sing So-lo-mon's.
last-ing keys And reigns as So-v'reign Lord.
ty and praise For all e-ter-ni-ty.

165 Ye That Know the Lord Is Gracious

... declare the wonderful deeds of him who called you/1 Pet 2:9

C A Alington (1872-1955)

Cyril Taylor (1907-   )
Abbot's Leigh   8 7 8 7 D

1. Ye that know the Lord is gra-cious, Ye for whom a
2. Liv-ing stones, by God ap-point-ed Each to his al-
3. Tell the praise of Him who called you Out of dark-ness

cor-ner stone Stands, of God e-lect and pre-cious, Laid that
lot-ted place, Kings and priests, by God a-noint-ed, Shall ye
in-to light, Broke the fet-ters that en-thralled you, Gave you

ye may build there-on, See that on that sure foun-
not de-clare His grace? Ye, a ro-yal gen-er-
free-dom, peace and sight: Tell the tale of sins for-

da-tion Ye a liv-ing tem-ple raise, Tow-ers that tell
a-tion, Tell the tid-ings of your birth, Tid-ings of a
giv-en, Strength re-newed and hope re-stored, Till the earth, in

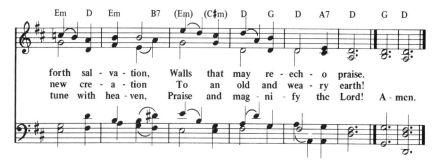

forth sal - va - tion, Walls that may re - ech - o praise.
new cre - a - tion To an old and wea - ry earth!
tune with hea - ven, Praise and mag - ni - fy the Lord! A - men.

music: from the BBC Hymn Book *by permission of Oxford University Press.*

166 Lord Jesus Christ, We Seek Thy Face   The Church

. . . let us draw near with a true heart/Heb 10:22

Alexander Stewart (1843-1923)

Leighton G Hayne (1836-1883)
St Lawrence 8 8 8 8

1. Lord Je - sus Christ, we seek Thy face, With in the veil we bow the knee;
2. We thank Thee for the pre-cious blood That purged our sins and brought us nigh,
3. Shut in with Thee, far, far a - bove The rest - less world that wars be - low,
4. The brow that once with thorns was bound, Thy hands, Thy side, we fain would see;

O, let Thy glo - ry fill the place, And bless us while we wait on Thee.
All cleansed and sanc - ti - fied, to God, Thy ho - ly name to mag - ni - fy.
We seek to learn and prove Thy love, Thy wis - dom and Thy grace to know.
Draw near, Lord Je - sus, glo - ry crowned, And bless us while we wait on Thee. A - men.

167 The Son of God Goes Forth to War

The Church

Are you able to drink the cup that I drink . . . ?/Mk 10:38

Reginald Heber (1783-1826)

Henry S Cutler (1824-1902)
All Saints, New   8 6 8 6 D

1. The Son of God goes forth to war, A king-ly crown to gain;
2. The mar-tyr first, whose ea-gle eye Could pierce be-yond the grave,
3. A glo-rious band, the cho-sen few On whom the Spi-rit came,
4. A no-ble ar-my, men and boys, The ma-tron and the maid,

His blood-red ban-ner streams a-far: Who fol-lows in His train?
Who saw his Mas-ter in the sky, And called on Him to save:
Twelve va-liant saints, their hope they knew, And mocked the cross and flame:
A-round the Sa-vior's throne re-joice, In robes of light ar-rayed:

Who best can drink his cup of woe, Tri-um-phant o-ver pain,
Like Him, with par-don on his tongue In midst of mor-tal pain,
They met the ty-rant's bran-dished steel, The li-on's go-ry mane;
They climbed the steep as-cent of heaven Through pe-ril, toil, and pain;

Who pa-tient bears his cross be-low, He fol-lows in His train.
He prayed for them that did the wrong: Who fol-lows in his train?
They bowed their necks the death to feel: Who fol-lows in their train?
O God, to us may grace be given To fol-low in their train. A-men.

168 Here, O My Lord

The Church

... let us draw near with a true heart in full assurance of faith/Heb 10:22

Horatius Bonar (1808-1889)

James Langran (1835-1909)
Langran 10 10 10 10

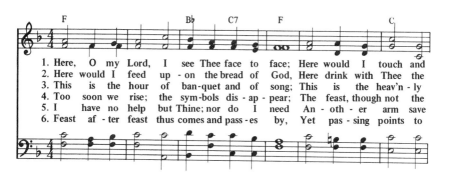

1. Here, O my Lord, I see Thee face to face; Here would I touch and
2. Here would I feed up-on the bread of God, Here drink with Thee the
3. This is the hour of ban-quet and of song; This is the heav'n-ly
4. Too soon we rise; the sym-bols dis-ap-pear; The feast, though not the
5. I have no help but Thine; nor do I need An-oth-er arm save
6. Feast af-ter feast thus comes and pass-es by, Yet pas-sing points to

han-dle things un-seen; Here grasp with firm-er hand th'e-ter-nal grace,
ro-yal wine of heav'n; Here would I lay a-side each earth-ly load,
ta-ble spread for me: Here let me feast, and feast-ing, still pro-long
love, is past and gone; The bread and wine re-move, but Thou art here,
Thine to lean up-on; It is e-nough, my Lord, e-nough in-deed;
the glad feast a-bove. Giv-ing sweet fore-taste of the fes-tal joy,

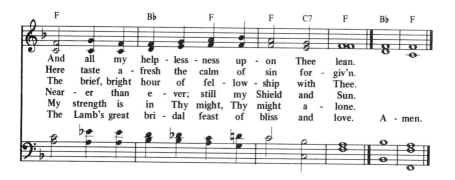

And all my help-less-ness up-on Thee lean.
Here taste a-fresh the calm of sin for-giv'n.
The brief, bright hour of fel-low-ship with Thee.
Near-er than e-ver; still my Shield and Sun.
My strength is in Thy might, Thy might a-lone.
The Lamb's great bri-dal feast of bliss and love. A-men.

Missions and Evangelism

Our God is gracious, infinite in mercy;
He bridged the hopeless gulf our sin had made;
He gave His Son to purchase our salvation—
In Jesus Christ we meet God unafraid!

Declare His glory among the nations;
Through all creation His triumph sing,
Till all earth's peoples bow in adoration
And Jesus Christ be everlasting King.

E Margaret Clarkson

169 Come, Ye Sinners

Missions & Evangelism

... him who comes to me I will not cast out/Jn 6:37

Joseph Hart (1712-1768)

William Owen (1814-1893)
Bryn Calfaria 8 7 8 7 12 7 7

1. Come, ye sin - ners, poor and wretch - ed, Weak and wound -ed, sick and sore;
2. Come, ye need - y, come, and wel - come; God's free boun - ty glo - ri - fy;
3. Come, ye wea - ry, hea - vy la - den, Bruised and bro - ken by the fall;
4. Let not con-science make you lin - ger, Nor of fit - ness fond - ly dream;
5. Lo! th'in - car - nate God a - scend - ed, Pleads the mer - it of His blood;

Je - sus read - y stands to save you, Full of pi - ty, joined with pow'r:
True be - lief and true re - pen - tance, E - v'ry grace that brings us nigh,
If you tar - ry till you're bet - ter, You will ne - ver come at all:
All the fit - ness He re - quir - eth Is to feel your need of Him:
Ven - ture on Him, ven - ture whol - ly; Let no oth - er trust in - trude:

He is a - ble, He is a - ble, He is a - ble,
With - out mon - ey, with - out mon - ey, with - out mon - ey,
Not the right - eous, not the right - eous, not the right - eous,
This He gives you; this He gives you; this He gives you;
None but Je - sus, none but Je - sus, none but Je - sus,

He is a - ble, He is a - ble, He is a - ble,

He is wil - ling, doubt no more. He is wil - ling, doubt no more.
Come to Je - sus Christ and buy. Come to Je - sus Christ and buy.
Sin - ners Je - sus came to call. Sin -ners Je - sus came to call.
'Tis the Spi - rit's ris - ing beam. 'Tis the Spi - rit's ris - ing beam.
Can do help - less sin - ners good. Can do help - less sin - ners good. A - men.

170 We Rest on Thee

... we rely on thee, and in thy name we have come/2 Chron 14:11

Edith G Cherry (1872-1897)

Jean Sibelius (1865-1957)
Finlandia 11 10 11 10 11 10

1. "We rest on Thee"—our Shield and our De - fen - der! We go not
2. Yea, "in Thy Name," O Cap - tain of sal - va - tion! In Thy dear
3. "We go" in faith, our own great weak-ness feel - ing, And need - ing
4. "We rest on Thee"—our Shield and our De - fen - der! Thine is the

forth a - lone a - gainst the foe; Strong in Thy strength, safe
Name, all oth - er names a - bove; Je - sus our Right - eous-
more each day Thy grace to know: Yet from our hearts a
bat - tle, Thine shall be the praise When pas- sing through the

in Thy keep - ing ten - der, "We rest on Thee, and
ness, our sure foun - da - tion, Our Prince of glo - ry
song of tri - umph peal - ing; "We rest on Thee, and
gates of pear - ly splen - dor, Vic - tors— we rest with

in Thy Name we go," Strong in Thy strength, safe in Thy keep - ing
and our King of love, Je - sus our Right - eous - ness our sure foun-
in Thy Name we go," Yet from our hearts a song of tri - umph
Thee, through end-less days, When pas - sing through the gates of pear - ly

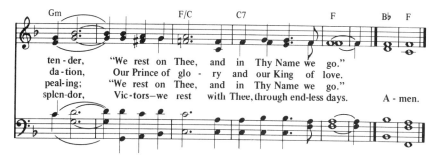

ten - der,   "We rest on Thee,   and in Thy Name we go."
da - tion,   Our Prince of glo - ry and our King of love.
peal - ing;   "We rest on Thee,   and in Thy Name we go."
splen - dor, Vic - tors—we rest   with Thee, through end - less days.   A - men.

melody: "Finlandia" by Jean Sibelius. Used by permission of Breitkopf & Hartel, Wiesbaden; arrangement copy © 1933 by the Presbyterian Board of Christian Education, renewed 1961; from The Hymnal; *used by permission of* The Westminster Press.

171 We Have Heard the Joyful   Missions & Evangelism
. . . all the ends of the earth shall see the salvation of . . . God/Is 52:10

Pricilla J Owens (1829-1907)

Josiah Booth (1852-1929)
Limpsfield / 3 / 3 / / / 3

1. We have heard the joy - ful sound; Je - sus saves! Spread the glad - ness
2. Sing a - bove the bat - tle strife; Je - sus saves! By His death and
3. Give the winds a might - y voice: Je - sus saves! Let the na - tions

all a - round; Je - sus saves! Bear the news to e - v'ry land, Climb the
end - less life, Je - sus saves! Sing it soft - ly through the gloom, When the
now re - joice: Je - sus saves! Sing ye is - lands of the sea; E - cho

steeps and cross the waves; On - ward! 'tis the Lord's com - mand: Je - sus saves!
heart for mer - cy craves; Sing in tri - umph o'er the tomb: Je - sus saves!
back ye o - cean caves; Shout sal - va - tion full and free: Je - sus saves!

music: from the Church Hymnary *by permission of Oxford University Press.*

172 All Authority and Power

Missions & Evangelism

All authority in heaven and on earth has been given to me/Mt 28:18

Christopher Idle (1938-   )

Joachim Neander (1650-1680)
descant by Hughes M Huffman (1942-   )
Unser Herrscher 8 7 8 7 8 7

1. All au - tho - ri - ty and pow - er, E - v'ry sta - tus and do - main,
2. All the na - tions owe Him wor - ship, E - v'ry tongue shall call Him Lord;
3. All the clear com-mands of Je - sus Must be heed - ed and o - beyed;
4. All the time He will be with us, Al - ways, to the end of days;

Now be - longs to Him who suf - fered Our re - demp - tion to ob - tain;
How are men to call up - on Him If His name they have not heard?
Full pro - vi - sion for our weak - ness In His teach - ing He has made;
With His own be - liev - ing peo - ple Who keep stead - fast in His ways;

An - gels, de - mons, kings and ru - lers, O - ver all shall Je - sus reign!
There-fore go and make dis - ci - ples, Preach His gos - pel, spread His Word.
In the Gos - pel words and sym - bols Sav - ing truth to us con-veyed.
God the Fa - ther, Son and Spi - rit, Bless us, and to Him the praise! A - men.

173 Soldiers of the Cross Arise

Missions & Evangelism

... and the sword of the Spirit, which is the word of God/Eph 6:17

William W How (1823-1897)

Medieval French Melody
Orientis Partibus 7 7 7 7

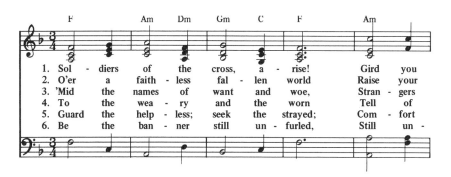

1. Sol - diers of the cross, a - rise! Gird you
2. O'er a faith - less fal - len world Raise your
3. 'Mid the names of want and woe, Stran - gers
4. To the wea - ry and the worn Tell of
5. Guard the help - less; seek the strayed; Com - fort
6. Be the ban - ner still un - furled, Still un -

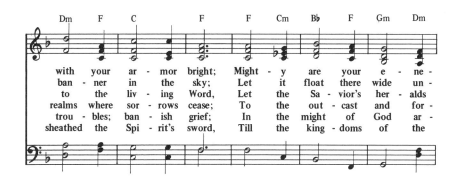

with your ar - mor bright; Might - y are your e - ne -
ban - ner in the sky; Let it float there wide un -
to the liv - ing Word, Let the Sa - vior's her - alds
realms where sor - rows cease; To the out - cast and for -
trou - bles; ban - ish grief; In the might of God ar -
sheathed the Spi - rit's sword, Till the king - doms of the

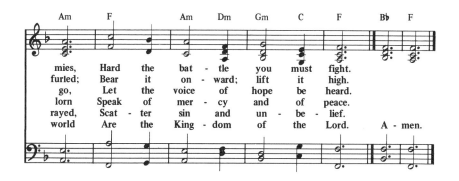

mies, Hard the bat - tle you must fight.
furled; Bear it on - ward; lift it high.
go, Let the voice of hope be heard.
lorn Speak of mer - cy and of peace.
rayed, Scat - ter sin and un - be - lief.
world Are the King - dom of the Lord. A - men.

174 Facing a Task Unfinished

Missions & Evangelism

And this gospel ... will be preached throughout the whole world/Mt 24:14

Frank Houghton (1894-1972)

Welsh Melody
Llangloffan 7 6 7 6 D

1. Fac - ing a task un - fin - ished, That drives us to our knees,
2. Where oth - er lords be - side thee Hold their un - hin - dered sway,
3. We bear the torch that flam - ing Fell from the hands of those
4. O Fa - ther, who sus - tained them, O Spi - rit, who in - spired,

A need that, un - di - min - ished, Re - bukes our sloth - ful ease,
Where for - ces that de - fied thee De - fy thee still to - day,
Who gave their lives pro - claim - ing That Je - sus died and rose;
Sa - vior, whose love con - strained them To toil with zeal un - tired,

We, who re - joice to know thee, Re - new be - fore thy throne
With none to heed their cry - ing For life and love and light,
Ours is the same com - mis - sion, The same glad mes - sage ours,
From co - war - dice de - fend us, From leth - ar - gy a - wake!

The sol - emn pledge we owe thee—To go and make thee known.
Un - num - bered souls are dy - ing, And pass in - to the night.
Fired by the same am - bi - tion, To thee we yield our pow'rs.
Forth on thy er - rands send us To la - bor for thy sake. A - men.

words: by permission of Mrs Frank Houghton.

175 Let God Be God

Missions & Evangelism

Blessed is the man who makes the LORD his trust/Ps 40:4

Bryan J Leech (1931-   )

Bryan J Leech (1931-   )
Carla 11 10 11 10

1. Let God be God, in this our pres - ent mo - ment,
2. Let God be God, or we shall ne - ver fin - ish
3. Let Christ be Lord, in all His ris - en po - wer;
4. Let this be ours as we a - wait His com - ing,

Let God be Mas - ter, hold-ing in con - trol   All parts of life as
The task to which He calls us e - v'ry day;   Lest er - ring we in
His gra - cious Spi - rit un - sup-pressed and free;   Our Fa - ther, re - cre -
To tell the World of Him our Lord and King.   O, let us march to

gifts of His be - stow - ment,   For mak - ing men now bro - ken,
un - be - lief di - min - ish   The force, the pow'r He wish - es
ate us for this hour   In - to the men you wish for
this, the dis - tant drum - ming   Which in cres-cen - do soon will

Coda (after vs. 4)

strong and whole.
to dis - play.
us to be.
roar and ring.   Let God be God, Let Christ be King!

176 Lord of the Universe

... all things were created through him and for him/Col 1:16

E Margaret Clarkson (1915-   )

E Margaret Clarkson (1915-   )
York Downs   10 10 10 10 D

1. Lord of the U - ni - verse, Hope of the world, Lord of the li - mit - less
2. Lord of the U - ni - verse, Hope of the world, Lord of the in - fi - nite
3. Lord of the U - ni - verse, Hope of the world, Send out Your light to the
4. Lord of the U - ni - verse, Hope of the world, How Your cre - a - tion cries

reach - es of space, Here on this pla - net You put on our flesh,
e - ons of time, You came a - mong us, lived our brief years,
ends of the earth; May we who know You o - bey Your com - mand,
out for re - lease! Looks for You, longs for You, wat - ches and waits,

Vast-ness con-fined in the womb of a maid, Born in our like - ness you
Tas - ted our griefs, our a - lone-ness, our fears, Con-quered our death, made e -
Go with the grace of Your gos - pel to all, Bring-ing sal - va - tion and
Prays for Your king-dom of jus - tice and peace! Mak - er, Re-deem - er, Tri -

ran - somed our race:
ter - ni - ty ours:
free - dom and joy: Sa - vior, we wor - ship You, praise and a - dore,
um - phant One, come!

Help us to hon-or You more and yet more, Help us to hon-or You more and yet more!

177 O Breath of Life

Wilt thou not revive us again . . . ?/Ps 85:6

Missions & Evangelism

Bessie P Head (1850-1936)

Mary J Hammond (1878-1964)
Spiritus Vitae 9 8 9 8

1. O Breath of Life, come sweep-ing through us, Re - vive Thy
2. O Wind of God, come bend us, break us, Till hum - bly
3. O Breath of Love, come breathe with - in us, Re - new - ing
4. Re - vive us, Lord! Is zeal a - bat - ing While har - vest

church with life and pow'r; O Breath of Life, come, cleanse, re -
we con - fess our need; Then in Thy ten - der - ness re -
thought and will and heart; Come, Love of Christ, a - fresh to
fields are vast and white? Re - vive us, Lord, the world is

new us, And fit Thy church to meet this hour.
make us, Re - vive, re - store, for this we plead.
win us, Re - vive Thy church in e - v'ry part.
wait - ing, E - quip Thy church to spread the light. A - men.

178 Declare His Glory

Declare his glory among the nations/Ps 96:3

E Margaret Clarkson (1915-   )

Donald P Hustad (1918-   )
Janus 11 10 11 10   w/refrain

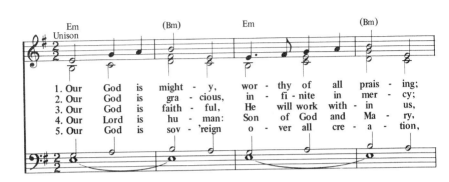

1. Our God is might - y, wor - thy of all prais - ing;
2. Our God is gra - cious, in - fi - nite in mer - cy;
3. Our God is faith - ful, He will work with - in us,
4. Our Lord is hu - man: Son of God and Ma - ry,
5. Our God is sov - 'reign o - ver all cre - a - tion,

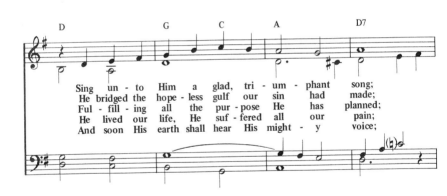

Sing un - to Him a glad, tri - um - phant song;
He bridged the hope - less gulf our sin had made;
Ful - fill - ing all the pur - pose He has planned;
He lived our life, He suf - fered all our pain;
And soon His earth shall hear His might - y voice;

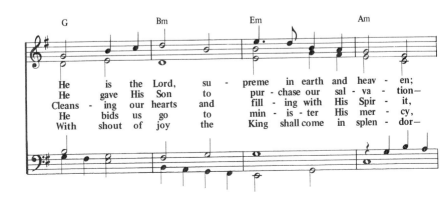

He is the Lord, su - preme in earth and heav - en;
He gave His Son to pur - chase our sal - va - tion—
Cleans - ing our hearts and fill - ing with His Spir - it,
He bids us go to min - is - ter His mer - cy,
With shout of joy the King shall come in splen - dor—

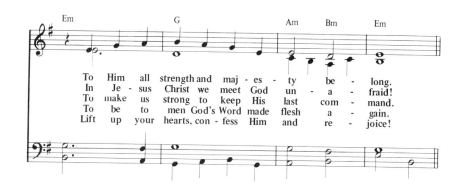

To Him all strength and maj - es - ty be - long.
In Je - sus Christ we meet God un - a - fraid!
To make us strong to keep His last com - mand.
To be to men God's Word made flesh a - gain.
Lift up your hearts, con - fess Him and re - joice!

Refrain

De - clare His glo - ry a - mong the na - tions; Through all cre -

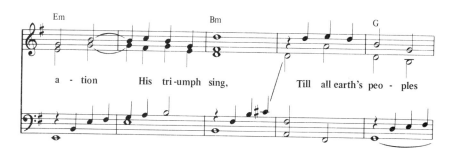

a - tion His tri - umph sing, Till all earth's peo - ples

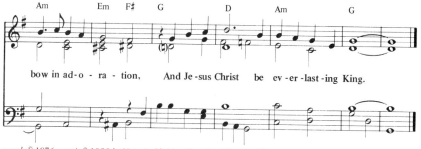

bow in ad - o - ra - tion, And Je - sus Christ be ev - er - last - ing King.

Morning and Evening

Awake, my soul, and with the sun
Thy daily stage of duty run;
Shake off dull sloth, and joyful rise
To pay thy morning sacrifice.
Thomas Ken

179 At Thy Feet, O Christ, We Lay

Morning & Evening

The LORD is your keeper/Ps 121:5

William Bright (1824-1901)

Welsh Melody
Arfon 7 7 7 7 7 7

1. At Thy feet, O Christ, we lay Thine own gift of
2. If it flow on calm and bright, Be Thy-self our
3. We in part our weak-ness know, And in part dis-
4. Fain would we Thy word em-brace, Live each mo-ment
5. Hear us, Lord, and that right soon; Hear, and grant the

this new day; Doubt of what it holds in store
chief de-light; If it bring un-known dis-tress,
cern our foe; Well for us, be-fore Thine eyes
on Thy grace, All our-selves to Thee con-sign,
choic-est boon That Thy love can e'er im-part,

Makes us crave Thine aid the more; Lest it prove a
Good is all that Thou canst bless; On-ly while its
All our dan-ger o-pen lies; Turn not from us
Fold up all our wills in Thine, Think, and speak, and
Loy-al sin-gle-ness of heart; So shall this and

time of loss, Mark it, Sa-vior, with Thy cross.
hours be-gin, Pray we, keep them clear of sin.
while we plead Thy com-pas-sions and our need.
do, and be Sim-ply that which pleas-es Thee.
all our days, Christ our God, show forth Thy praise. A-men.

180 Glory to Thee, My God

In peace I will both lie down and sleep/Ps 4:8

Thomas Ken (1637-1711)

Thomas Tallis (c1505-1585)
Tallis Canon 8 8 8 8

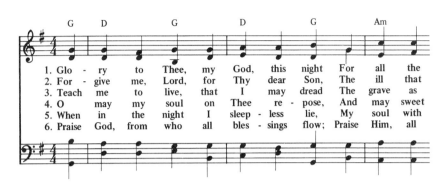

1. Glo - ry to Thee, my God, this night For all the
2. For - give me, Lord, for Thy dear Son, The ill that
3. Teach me to live, that I may dread The grave as
4. O may my soul on Thee re - pose, And may sweet
5. When in the night I sleep - less lie, My soul with
6. Praise God, from who all bles - sings flow; Praise Him, all

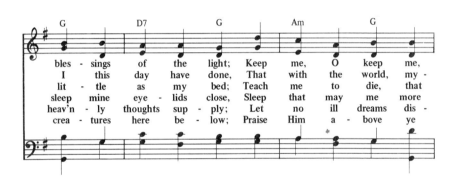

bles - sings of the light; Keep me, O keep me,
I this day have done, That with the world, my -
lit - tle as my bed; Teach me to die, that
sleep mine eye - lids close, Sleep that may me more
heav'n - ly thoughts sup - ply; Let no ill dreams dis -
crea - tures here be - low; Praise Him a - bove ye

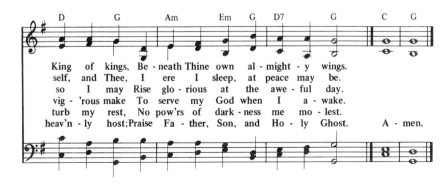

King of kings, Be - neath Thine own al - might - y wings.
self, and Thee, I ere I sleep, at peace may be.
so I may Rise glo - rious at the awe - ful day.
vig - 'rous make To serve my God when I a - wake.
turb my rest, No pow'rs of dark - ness me mo - lest.
heav'n - ly host; Praise Fa - ther, Son, and Ho - ly Ghost. A - men.

181 Awake, My Soul

I will awake the dawn! I will give thanks to thee, O LORD/Ps 108:2, 3

Thomas Ken (1637-1711)

Francois H Barthelemon (1741-1808)
Morning Hymn 8 8 8 8

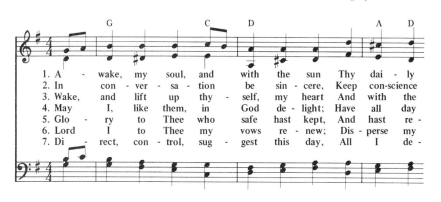

1. A - wake, my soul, and with the sun Thy dai - ly
2. In con - ver - sa - tion be sin - cere, Keep con-science
3. Wake, and lift up thy - self, my heart And with the
4. May I, like them, in God de - light; Have all day
5. Glo - ry to Thee who safe hast kept, And hast re -
6. Lord I to Thee my vows re - new; Dis - perse my
7. Di - rect, con - trol, sug - gest this day, All I de -

stage of du - ty run; Shake off dull sloth, and
as the noon - day clear; Think how all see - ing
an - gels bear thy part, Who all night long un -
long my God in sight! Per - form, like them, my
freshed me whilst I slept; Grant, Lord, when I from
sins as mor - ning dew; Guard my first springs of
sign or do, or say; That all my pow'rs, with

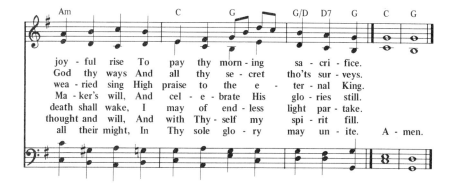

joy - ful rise To pay thy morn - ing sa - cri - fice.
God thy ways And all thy se - cret tho'ts sur - veys.
wea - ried sing High praise to the e - ter - nal King.
Ma - ker's will, And cel - e - brate His glo - ries still.
death shall wake, I may of end - less light par - take.
thought and will, And with Thy - self my spi - rit fill.
all their might, In Thy sole glo - ry may un - ite. A - men.

182 Come, My Soul

Awake, my soul! . . . I will awake the dawn!/Ps 57:8

F R L von Canitz
tr H J Buckoll

Franz J Haydn (1732-1809)
Haydn 8 4 7 8 4 7

1. Come, my soul, thou must be wak - ing; Now is break - ing O'er the earth an - oth - er day: Come to Him who made this splen - dor; See thou ren - der All thy fee - ble strength can pay.

2. Glad - ly hail the sun re - turn - ing; Read - y burn - ing Be the in - cense of thy pow'rs; For the night is safe - ly end - ed; God hath tend - ed With His care thy help - less hours.

3. Pray that He may pro - sper ev - er Each en - dea - vor, When thine aim is good and true; But that He may e - ver thwart thee, And con - vert thee, When thou e - vil wouldst pur - sue.

4. Our God's boun - teous gifts a - buse not, Light re - fuse not, But His Spi - rit's voice o - bey; Thou with Him shalt dwell, be - hold - ing Light en - fold - ing All things in un - cloud - ed day. A - men.

183 The Day Thou Gavest, Lord

Morning & Evening

From the rising of the sun to its setting ... the LORD ... be praised/Ps 113:3

John Ellerton (1826-1893)

Clement C Scholefield (1839-1904)
St Clement 9 8 9 8

1. The day Thou ga - vest, Lord, is end - ed, The dark - ness
2. We thank Thee that Thy Church un - sleep - ing, While earth rolls
3. As o'er each con - ti - nent and is - land The dawn leads
4. So be it Lord; Thy throne shall ne - ver, Like earth's proud

falls at Thy be - hest; To Thee our morn - ing hymns a -
on - ward in - to light, Through all the world her watch is
on an - oth - er day, The voice of prayer is ne - ver
em - pires, pass a - way; Thy king - dom stands, and grows for

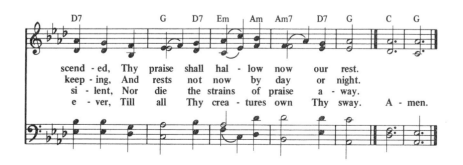

scend - ed, Thy praise shall hal - low now our rest.
keep - ing, And rests not now by day or night.
si - lent, Nor die the strains of praise a - way.
e - ver, Till all Thy crea - tures own Thy sway. A - men.

184 At Even, Ere the Sun Was Set

That evening, at sundown, they brought to him all who were sick/Mk 1:32

Henry Twells (1823-1900)

Georg Joseph (c 1650)
Angelus 8 8 8 8

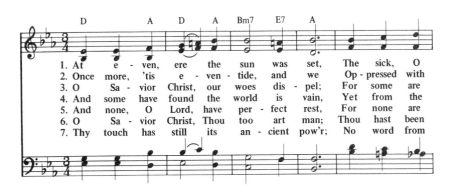

1. At   e - ven,   ere   the   sun   was   set,   The   sick,   O
2. Once   more,   'tis   e - ven - tide,   and   we   Op - pressed   with
3. O   Sa - vior   Christ,   our   woes   dis - pel;   For   some   are
4. And   some   have   found   the   world   is   vain,   Yet   from   the
5. And   none,   O   Lord,   have   per - fect   rest,   For   none   are
6. O   Sa - vior   Christ,   Thou   too   art   man;   Thou   hast   been
7. Thy   touch   has   still   its   an - cient   pow'r;   No   word   from

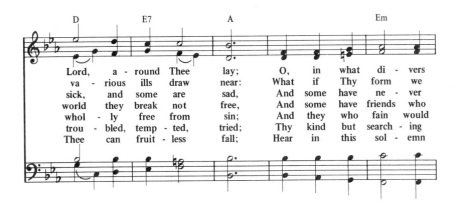

Lord,   a - round   Thee   lay;   O,   in   what   di - vers
va - rious   ills   draw   near: What   if   Thy   form   we
sick,   and   some   are   sad,   And   some   have   ne - ver
world   they   break   not   free,   And   some   have   friends   who
whol - ly   free   from   sin;   And   they   who   fain   would
trou - bled,   temp - ted,   tried;   Thy   kind   but   search - ing
Thee   can   fruit - less   fall;   Hear   in   this   sol - emn

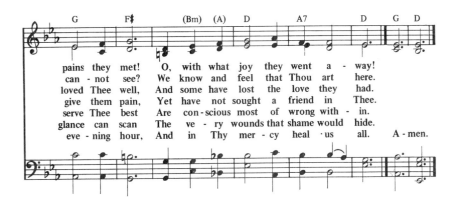

pains   they   met!   O,   with   what   joy   they   went   a - way!
can - not   see?   We   know   and   feel   that   Thou   art   here.
loved   Thee   well,   And   some   have   lost   the   love   they   had.
give   them   pain,   Yet   have   not   sought   a   friend   in   Thee.
serve   Thee   best   Are   con - scious   most   of   wrong   with - in.
glance   can   scan   The   ve - ry   wounds   that   shame   would   hide.
eve - ning   hour,   And   in   Thy   mer - cy   heal ·us   all.   A - men.

185 Savior, Breathe an Evening

You will not fear the terror of the night/Ps 91:5

Morning & Evening

James Edmeston (1791-1867)

George C Stebbins (1846-1945)
Sunset   8 7 8 7

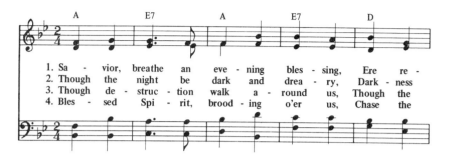

1. Sa - vior, breathe an eve - ning bles - sing, Ere re -
2. Though the night be dark and drea - ry, Dark - ness
3. Though de - struc - tion walk a - round us, Though the
4. Bles - sed Spi - rit, brood - ing o'er us, Chase the

pose our spi - rits seal; Sin and want we
can - not hide from Thee; Thou art He who,
ar - row past us fly, An - gel guards from
dark - ness of our night, Till the per - fect

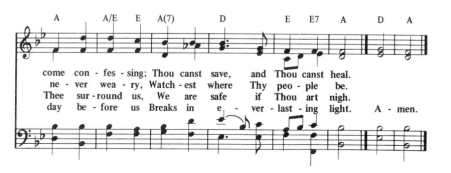

come con - fes - sing; Thou canst save, and Thou canst heal.
ne - ver wea - ry, Watch - est where Thy peo - ple be.
Thee sur - round us, We are safe if Thou art nigh.
day be - fore us Breaks in e - ver - last - ing light. A - men.

Psalms

As the deer longs for water
My soul longs for You, Lord,
My soul is thirsty for the living God—
I long to see His face.
Through the day He shows mercy,
And so, in the evening,
I sing to Him with praise upon my lips—
In my life He is God.

Michael Baughen

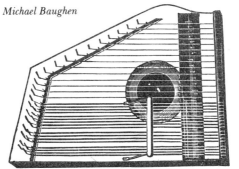

186 God Is Our Strength and Refuge

God is our refuge and strength/Ps 46:1

Richard Bewes

arr Marc Hedlin (1942-   )
Dambusters' March   7 7 7 5 7 8 11

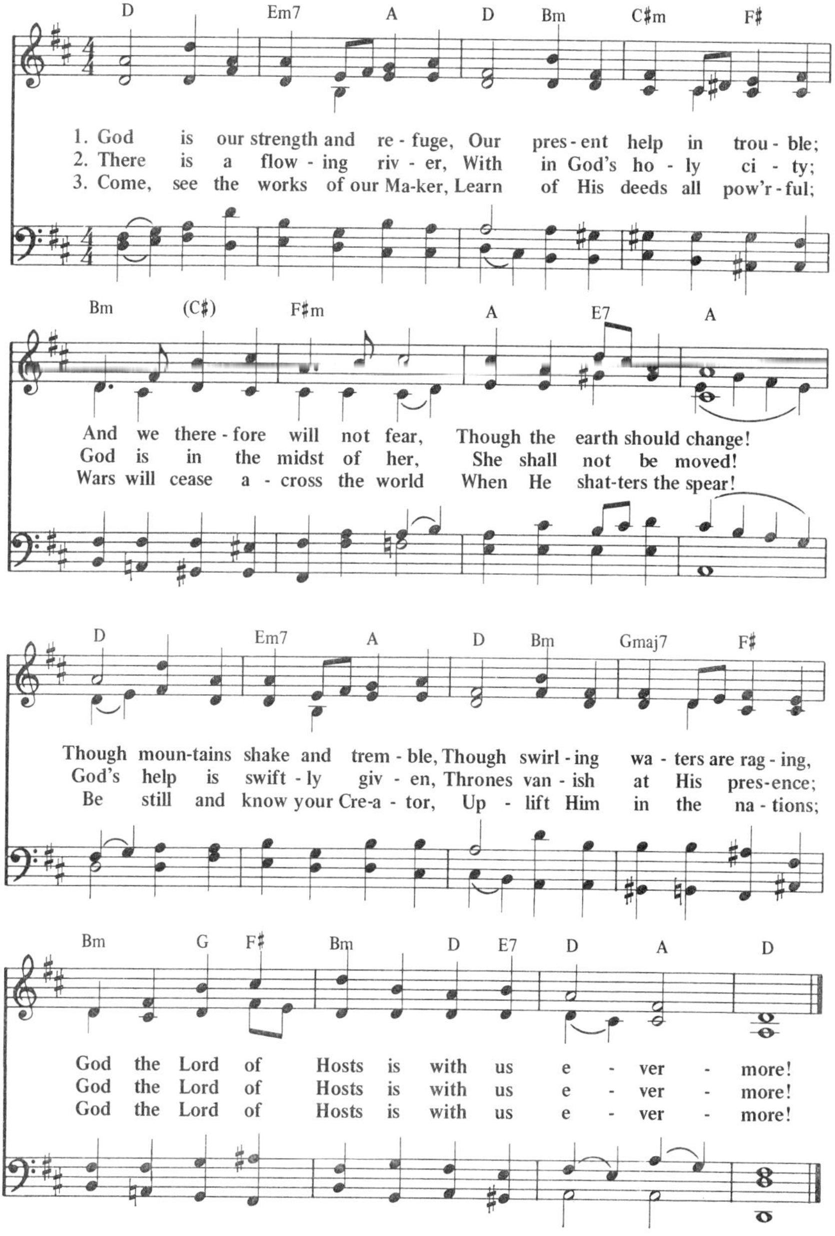

D Em7 A D Bm C♯m F♯
1. God is our strength and re - fuge, Our pres - ent help in trou - ble;
2. There is a flow - ing riv - er, With in God's ho - ly ci - ty;
3. Come, see the works of our Ma-ker, Learn of His deeds all pow'r - ful;
Bm (C♯) F♯m A E7 A
And we there - fore will not fear, Though the earth should change!
God is in the midst of her, She shall not be moved!
Wars will cease a - cross the world When He shat-ters the spear!
D Em7 A D Bm Gmaj7 F♯
Though moun-tains shake and trem - ble, Though swirl - ing wa - ters are rag - ing,
God's help is swift - ly giv - en, Thrones van - ish at His pres-ence;
Be still and know your Cre-a - tor, Up - lift Him in the na - tions;
Bm G F♯ Bm D E7 D A D
God the Lord of Hosts is with us e - ver - more!
God the Lord of Hosts is with us e - ver - more!
God the Lord of Hosts is with us e - ver - more!

187 The God of Love My Shepherd Is

The LORD is my shepherd/Ps 23:1

George Herbert (1593-1632)

von Spee's "Trutz Nachtigall" Cologne (1649)
harm Anthony Hedges (1931-   )
Nachtigall 8 7 8 7 D iambic

1. The God of love my Shep-herd is, And He that doth me
3. Or if I stray, He doth con-vert, And bring my mind in

feed: While He is mine and I am His, What can I
frame: And all this not for my de-sert, But for His

want or need?
ho-ly Name.

2. He leads me to the ten-der grass, Where
4. Yea, in death's sha-dy, black a-bode Well
5. Sure-ly Thy sweet and won-drous love Shall

I both feed and rest; Then to the streams that gent-ly
may I walk, not fear, For Thou art with me, and Thy
mea-sure all my days; And as it ne-ver shall re-

pass, In both I have the best.
rod To guide, Thy staff to bear. *D. S.*
move, So nei - ther shall my praise. A - men.

188 The Lord's My Shepherd, I'll Not Want

Psalms

The LORD is my shepherd/Ps 23:1

"Scottish Psalter" (1650)

Jessie S Irvine (1836-1887)
harmonized by T C L Pritchard (1885-1960)
Crimond 8 6 8 6

1. The Lord's my Shep - herd, I'll not want; He makes me down to
2. My soul He doth re - store a - gain; And me to walk doth
3. Yea, though I walk through death's dark vale, Yet will I fear no
4. My ta - ble Thou hast fur - nish - ed In pres - ence of my
5. Good - ness and mer - cy all my life Shall sure - ly fol - low

lie In pas - tures green; He lead - eth me The qui - et wa - ters by.
make With in the paths of right - eous - ness, E'en for His own name's sake.
ill; For Thou art with me, and Thy rod And staff me com - fort still.
foes; My head Thou dost with oil a - noint, And my cup o - ver - flows.
me; And in God's house for - e - ver - more My dwel - ling place shall be.

from the Scottish Psalter *by permission of Oxford University Press.*

189 Call Jehovah Thy Salvation

My refuge and my fortress; my God, in whom I trust/Ps 91:2

James Montgomery (1771-1854)

Rowland H Prichard (1811-1887)
harmonized by David Evans (1874-1948)
Hyfrydol 8 7 8 7 D

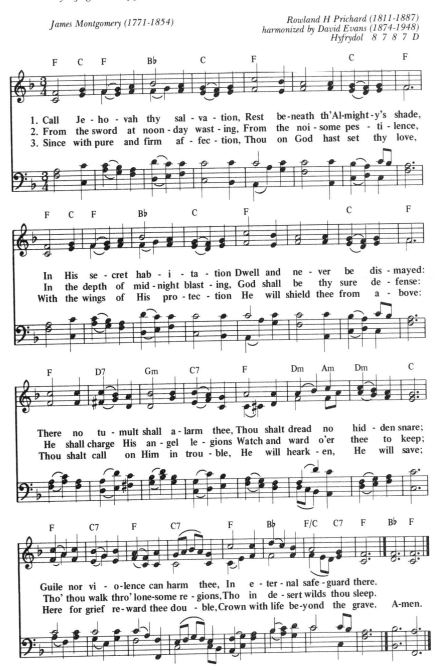

1. Call Je-ho-vah thy sal-va-tion, Rest be-neath th'Al-might-y's shade.
2. From the sword at noon-day wast-ing, From the noi-some pes-ti-lence,
3. Since with pure and firm af-fec-tion, Thou on God hast set thy love,

In His se-cret hab-i-ta-tion Dwell and ne-ver be dis-mayed.
In the depth of mid-night blast-ing, God shall be thy sure de-fense;
With the wings of His pro-tec-tion He will shield thee from a-bove:

There no tu-mult shall a-larm thee, Thou shalt dread no hid-den snare;
He shall charge His an-gel le-gions Watch and ward o'er thee to keep;
Thou shalt call on Him in trou-ble, He will heark-en, He will save;

Guile nor vi-o-lence can harm thee, In e-ter-nal safe-guard there.
Tho' thou walk thro' lone-some re-gions, Tho in de-sert wilds thou sleep.
Here for grief re-ward thee dou-ble, Crown with life be-yond the grave. A-men.

music: from the Revised Church Hymnary 1927 *by permission of Oxford University Press.*

190 Safe in the Shadow of the Lord

Psalms

... under his wings you will find refuge/Ps 91:4

Timothy Dudley-Smith

Norman Warren (1934-   )
8 7 8 6

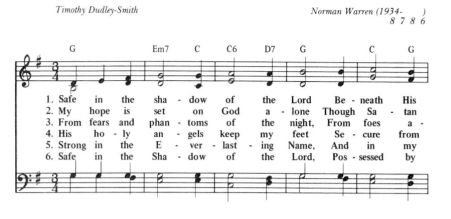

1. Safe in the sha - dow of the Lord Be - neath His
2. My hope is set on God a - lone Though Sa - tan
3. From fears and phan - toms of the night, From foes a -
4. His ho - ly an - gels keep my feet Se - cure from
5. Strong in the E - ver - last - ing Name, And in my
6. Safe in the Sha - dow of the Lord, Pos - sessed by

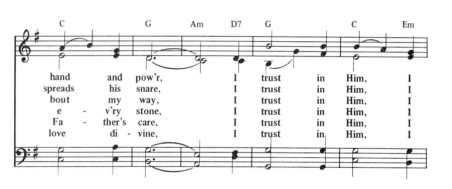

hand and pow'r, I trust in Him, I
spreads his snare, I trust in Him, I
bout my way, I trust in Him, I
e - v'ry stone, I trust in Him, I
Fa - ther's care, I trust in Him, I
love di - vine, I trust in Him, I

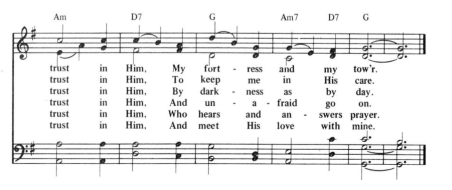

trust in Him, My fort - ress and my tow'r.
trust in Him, To keep me in His care.
trust in Him, By dark - ness as by day.
trust in Him, And un - a - fraid go on.
trust in Him, Who hears and an - swers prayer.
trust in Him, And meet His love with mine.

191 Unto the Hills Around Do I Lift Up

Psalms

I lift up my eyes to the hills. From whence does my help come?/Ps 121:1

John D S Campbell (1845-1914)

Charles Purday (1779-1885)
Sandon 10 4 10 4 10 10

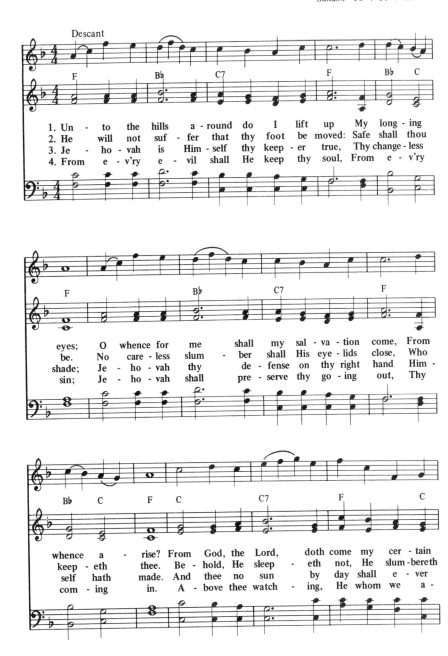

1. Un - to the hills a - round do I lift up My long - ing
2. He will not suf - fer that thy foot be moved: Safe shall thou
3. Je - ho - vah is Him - self thy keep - er true, Thy change - less
4. From e - v'ry e - vil shall He keep thy soul, From e - v'ry

eyes; O whence for me shall my sal - va - tion come, From
be. No care - less slum - ber shall His eye - lids close, Who
shade; Je - ho - vah thy de - fense on thy right hand Him -
sin; Je - ho - vah shall pre - serve thy go - ing out, Thy

whence a - rise? From God, the Lord, doth come my cer - tain
keep - eth thee. Be - hold, He sleep - eth not, He slum - bereth
self hath made. And thee no sun by day shall e - ver
com - ing in. A - bove thee watch - ing, He whom we a -

aid, From God, the Lord, who heav'n and earth hath made.
ne'er, Who keep - eth Is - rael in His ho - ly care.
smite; No moon shall harm thee in the si - lent night.
dore Shall keep thee hence - forth, yea, for - e - ver - more. A - men.

192 Mercy, Blessing, Favor, Grace

Psalms

May God be gracious to us and bless us/Ps 67:1

Timothy Dudley-Smith

David G Wilson
7 7 7 7

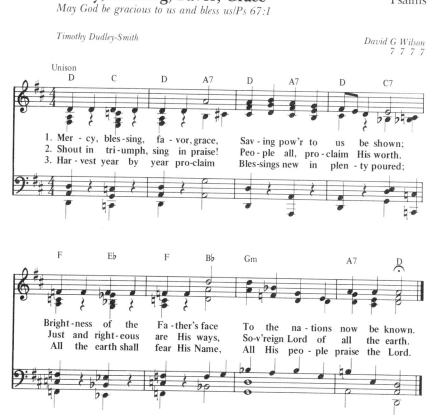

1. Mer - cy, bles - sing, fa - vor, grace, Sav - ing pow'r to us be shown;
2. Shout in tri - umph, sing in praise! Peo - ple all, pro - claim His worth.
3. Har - vest year by year pro - claim Bles-sings new in plen - ty poured;

Bright - ness of the Fa - ther's face To the na - tions now be known.
Just and right - eous are His ways, So-v'reign Lord of all the earth.
All the earth shall fear His Name, All His peo - ple praise the Lord.

193 Sing a New Song to the Lord

Psalms

O sing to the LORD a new song/Ps 98:1

Timothy Dudley-Smith

David Wilson
7 7 11 8

1. Sing a new song to the Lord, He to whom won-ders be-
   long! Re - joice in His tri - umph and
   tell of His pow'r; O sing to the
   Lord a new song!

2. Now to the ends of the earth See His sal - va - tion is
   shown: And still He re - mem - bers His
   mer - cy and truth, Un - chang - ing in
   love to His own.

3. Sing a new song and re - joice, Pub - lish His prais - es a-
   broad! Let voic - es in cho - rus, with
   trum - pet and horn, Re - sound for the
   joy of the Lord!

4. Join with the hills and the sea Thun - ders of praise to pro-
   long! In judge - ment and jus - tice He
   comes to the earth; O sing to the
   Lord a new song!

Vs. 1, 2, 3 | Last Verse

194 The God of Heaven Thunders

Psalms

The voice of the LORD is upon the waters/Ps 29:3

Michael Perry

Norman Warren (1934-)
7 7 7 5 6

1. The God of hea - ven thun - ders, His voice in ca - dent
2. The des - ert writhes in tem - pest, Wind whips the trees to
3. The might - y God e - ter - nal Is to His throne a -

e - choes Re - sounds a - bove the wa - ters,
fu - ry, Sear light - ning splits the for - est
scend - ed, And we who are His peo - ple,

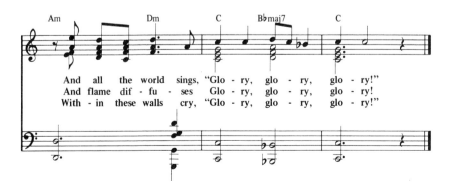

And all the world sings, "Glo - ry, glo - ry, glo - ry!"
And flame dif - fu - ses Glo - ry, glo - ry, glo - ry!
With - in these walls cry, "Glo - ry, glo - ry, glo - ry!"

195 The God of Heaven Thunders

The voice of the LORD is upon the waters/Ps 29:3

Michael Perry

Norman Warren (1934-   )

7 7 7 5 6

1. The God of hea - ven thun - ders, (thun - ders,) His voice in ca - dent
2. The des - ert writhes in tem - pest, (tem - pest,) Wind whips the trees to
3. The might - y God e - ter - nal (eter - nal) Is to His throne a -

e - choes (e - choes) Re - sounds a - bove the wa - ters, (wa - ters,)
fu - ry, (fu - ry,) Sear light - ning splits the fo - rest (fo - rest)
scend - ed, (ascend - ed,) And we who are His peo - ple, (peo - ple,)

1. And all the world sings, 'Glo - ry, glo - ry, glo - ry!'
2. And flame dif - fu - ses

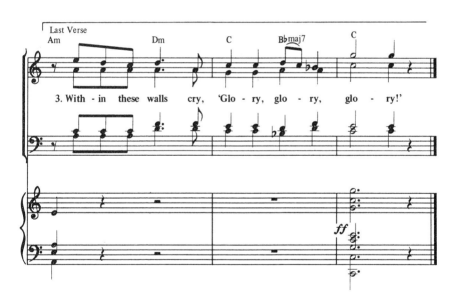

3. With - in these walls cry, 'Glo - ry, glo - ry, glo - ry!'

196 In Silence My Soul Is Waiting

Psalms

For God alone my soul waits in silence/Ps 62:1

Michael Saward (1932-   )

Christian Strover
8 7 8 7 8 7

1. In si - lence my soul is wait - ing, Is wait - ing for
2. You set on a man and you beat him, The pack of you
3. You plot for his un - der - min - ing, You slan - der him
4. Be si - lent, my soul, in wait - ing, In wait - ing for
5. There's safe - ty in God, and hon - or, My re - fuge, my
6. Just puffs of the wind, the peo - ple, Great men are il -
7. Don't trust, then, in cruel ex - tor - tion, Don't plun - der, de -
8. U - nique - ly, our God has spo - ken, Of two things I've

God a - lone, De - liv'- rance from Him is com - ing, My
knock him down, As a tot - ter - ing wall he stag - gers, Sub-
with your lies, You love, with faint praise, to damn him, Sweet
God a - lone, As - su - rance from Him is com - ing, My
rock, my strength, So hide in our God, you peo - ple, And
lu - sions, all, As breath in the air, they're mea - sured, Then
fraud and steal, Don't set your heart on pos - ses - sions, E -
heard Him speak— He's the source of pow'r and mer - cy, To

res - cu - er, fort and rock. In si - lence my soul is
sides like a sag - ging fence. In si - lence my soul is
tongued, you've a curse - filled heart. In si - lence my soul is
res - cu - er, fort and rock. Be si - lent, my soul, in
pour out your hearts to Him. Be si - lent, my soul, in
weight - less they fade a - way. Be si - lent, my soul, in
spe - cially if they in - crease. Be si - lent, my soul, in
men He re - pays their deeds. Be si - lent, my soul, in

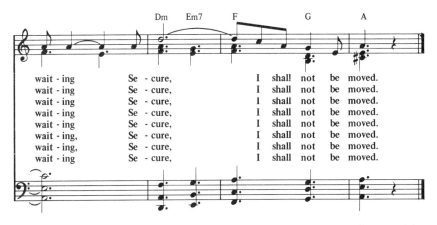

wait - ing   Se - cure,   I shall not be moved.
wait - ing   Se - cure,   I shall not be moved.
wait - ing   Se - cure,   I shall not be moved.
wait - ing   Se - cure,   I shall not be moved.
wait - ing   Se - cure,   I shall not be moved.
wait - ing,   Se - cure,   I shall not be moved.
wait - ing,   Se - cure,   I shall not be moved.
wait - ing   Se - cure,   I shall not be moved.

197 O God, Our Help in Ages Past

Psalms

Lord, thou hast been our dwelling place in all generations/Ps 90:1

Isaac Watts (1674-1748)

William Croft (1678-1727)
St Anne 8 6 8 6

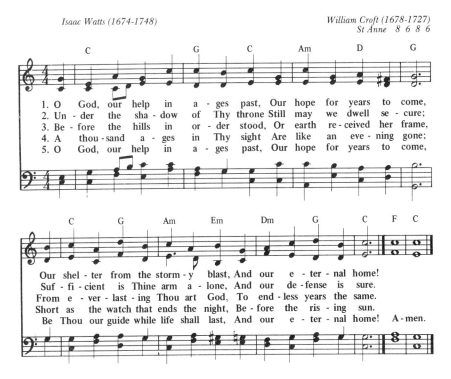

1. O God, our help in a - ges past, Our hope for years to come,
2. Un - der the sha - dow of Thy throne Still may we dwell se - cure;
3. Be - fore the hills in or - der stood, Or earth re - ceived her frame,
4. A thou - sand a - ges in Thy sight Are like an eve - ning gone;
5. O God, our help in a - ges past, Our hope for years to come,

Our shel - ter from the storm - y blast, And our e - ter - nal home!
Suf - fi - cient is Thine arm a - lone, And our de - fense is sure.
From e - ver - last - ing Thou art God, To end - less years the same.
Short as the watch that ends the night, Be - fore the ris - ing sun.
Be Thou our guide while life shall last, And our e - ter - nal home! A - men.

198 Blessed Is the Man

Blessed is the man who walks not in the counsel of the wicked/Ps 1:1

Michael Baughen

Michael Baughen
arr Jim Thornton
11 14 12 12 8 8

light, by day and night, Is the law of God Al - might - y.
light, by day and night, Is the law of God Al - might - y.
way of right-eous men And un - god - ly ways will per - ish.

D. S. al Fine

199 O God, May Your Face Ever Shine

Psalms

May God ... make his face to shine upon us/Ps 67:1

Douglas Thornton

Traditional melody
arr Norman Warren (1934-   )
11 8 11 9

1. O God, may Your face e - ver shine up - on men And be
2. We pray that Your way may be known on the earth And the
3. We pray that the peo - ple may joy - ful - ly sing For You
4. O God, we give thanks for Your bles - sings to us, You have

gra - cious and swift to bless; Then let all the world come and
might of Your sav - ing pow'r; Then let all the world come and
rule as a right - eous judge; Then let all the world come and
fed us from earth's har - vest fields; So let all the world come and

praise You, O Lord, All the peo - ple on earth give You praise.
praise You, O Lord, All the peo - ple on earth give You praise.
praise You, O Lord, All the peo - ple on earth give You praise.
thank You, O Lord, All the peo - ple on earth give You praise.

200 In Majesty and Splendor

Psalms

Thou art clothed with honor and majesty/Ps 104:1

Michael Perry

Norman Warren (1934-   )
7 6 7 6 D

1. In ma - jes - ty and splen - dor And
2. The earth You set se - cure - ly And
3. To men You give the har - vest, Give
4. You spread the shades of dark - ness, You
5. The bounds of Your cre - a - tion—They

robes of light en - dowed Is God who spreads the
cov - ered with a cloak Of wa - ters o - ver
a - ni - mals to feed, To e - v'ry sup-pliant
forge the day-time heat, You teach the moon the
can - not be ap - prised, And count - less are the

hea - vens And rides up - on the cloud. With
moun - tains Which, at your bid - ding, broke And,
crea - ture The grac - es that we need. The
sea - sons, The sun to rise and set. For
won - ders Your wis - dom has de - vised. Yet

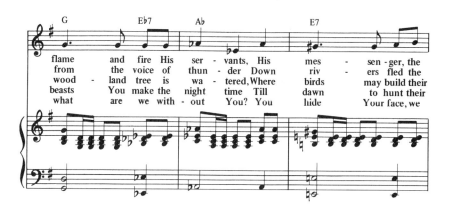

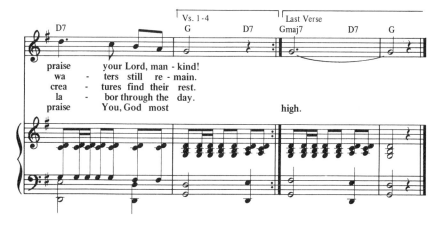

201 God Is Our Refuge

Psalms

God is our refuge and strength/Ps 46:1

Psalm 46:1, 2, 6

Stanley Houghton (1900-1950)
Irregular

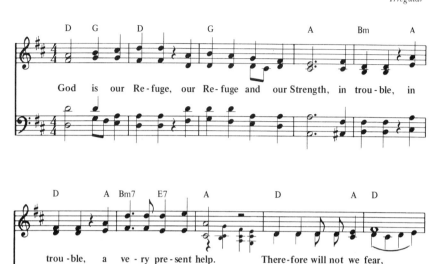

God is our Re-fuge, our Re-fuge and our Strength, in trou-ble, in

trou-ble, a ve-ry pre-sent help. There-fore will not we fear,

There-fore, will not we fear; The Lord of Hosts is with us, The

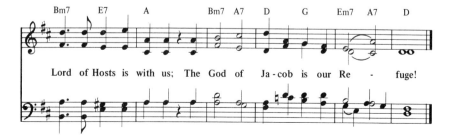

Lord of Hosts is with us; The God of Ja-cob is our Re - fuge!

202 I Lift My Eyes

Psalms

I lift my eyes to the hills. From whence does my help come?/Ps 121:1

Timothy Dudley-Smith

Michael Baughen
Elizabeth Crocker
4 5 8 4 5 7

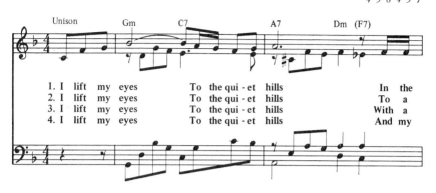

1. I lift my eyes To the qui - et hills In the press of the bu - sy day;
2. I lift my eyes To the qui - et hills To a calm that is mine to share;
3. I lift my eyes To the qui - et hills With a prayer as I turn to sleep;
4. I lift my eyes To the qui - et hills And my heart to the Fa - ther's throne;

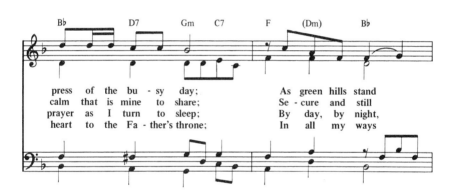

As green hills stand Se - cure and still By day, by night, In all my ways

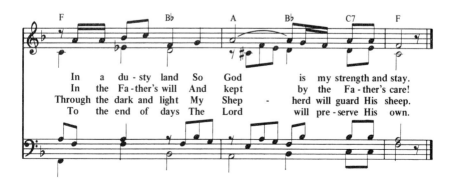

In a du - sty land So God is my strength and stay.
In the Fa - ther's will And kept by the Fa - ther's care!
Through the dark and light My Shep - herd will guard His sheep.
To the end of days The Lord will pre - serve His own.

203 I Lift My Eyes

Psalms

I lift my eyes to the hills. From whence does my help come?/Ps 121:1

Timothy Dudley-Smith

Michael Baughen
Elizabeth Crocker
4 5 8 4 5 7

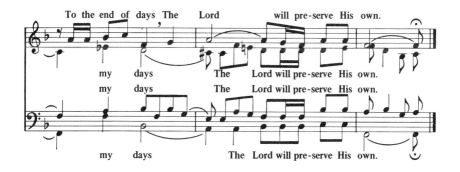

204 As the Deer Longs for Water

Psalms

As a hart longs for flowing streams, so longs my soul for thee/Ps 42:1

Michael Baughen

Michael Baughen
arr David Wilson
7 6 10 6

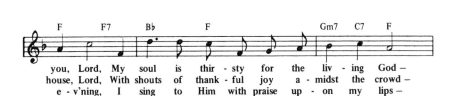

1. As the deer longs for wa - ter My soul longs for
2. In the past I was lead - ing The praise in your
3. Thru the day He shows mer - cy, And so, in the

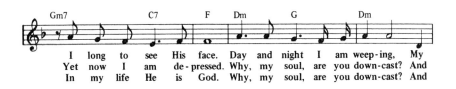

you, Lord, My soul is thir - sty for the liv - ing God —
house, Lord, With shouts of thank - ful joy a - midst the crowd —
e - v'ning, I sing to Him with praise up - on my lips —

I long to see His face. Day and night I am weep-ing, My
Yet now I am de - pressed. Why, my soul, are you down-cast? And
In my life He is God. Why, my soul, are you down-cast? And

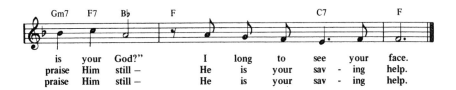

soul is poured out, Lord, Each day I hear it said, "Where
why are you groan - ing? Re - new your hope in God, and
why are you groan - ing? Re - new your hope in God, and

is your God?" I long to see your face.
praise Him still — He is your sav - ing help.
praise Him still — He is your sav - ing help.

Indexes

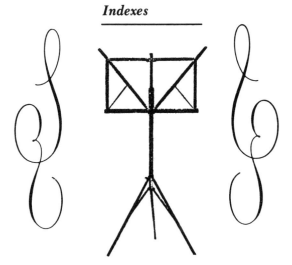